SOUND ANATOMIZ'D,

IN A

Philosophical ESSAY

ON

MUSICK.

Wherein is explained
The Nature of SOUND, both in its ESSENCE
and REGULATION, &c. Contrived for the Use
of the VOICE in SINGING, as well as for those
who Play on INSTRUMENTS.

Together with
A thorough Explanation of all the different
MOODS used in MUSICK, for regulating TIME
in the different Divisions of MEASURES used
therein.
All render'd plain and easy, to the meanest
CAPACITIES, by familiar SIMILIES.

To which is added,
A DISCOURSE, concerning the ABUSE of MUSICK.

By WILLIAM TURNER.

LONDON,
Printed by WILLIAM PEARSON, over-against
Wright's-Coffee-House, in *Aldersgate-street*, for the AUTHOR,
and Sold by M. TURNER, at the *Post-House*, in *Russel-street*, *Covent-Garden*, and no where else in *England*. 1724.

Monuments of Music and Music Literature
in
Facsimile

Second Series—Music Literature
CXXVII

SOUND ANATOMIZ'D

William Turner *fl. 18th century.*

Sound Anatomiz'd,
in a
Philosophical Essay
on
Musick

A Facsimile of the London, 1724 Edition

Broude Brothers Limited
New York

ISBN 0-8450-2327-6

Printed in U.S.A., 1974

PREFACE.

*A*mong the numerous Treatises that have been writ upon Musick, for the instructing of People in the Practise thereof, I have not yet met with any that have treated so fully on the Subject, as to render it so plain and intelligible, but that there is still Ground-work enough remaining for a farther Explanation; which is the Design of the following Sheets, to treat of it in such a familiar Way, as may let the Reader into the Marrow of it; who, when he shall see it dissected, will be the better able to form a just Idea, by being told the true Meaning of every Thing in its natural Course, which is undoubtedly the best Method that can be taken; for when he is made acquainted with the Reasons of Things, deduced from their proper Causes, he'll know the better how to make a right Application.

I am

Preface.

I am very sensible that there are much abler Hands *to undertake such a* Work; *but, as none have yet obliged the* World *with their Performances, I hope they'll pardon me for appearing in this Manner; for, being but too conscious of my own Inabilities, I cannot but expect to be censur'd by those who will immediately discover whatever Defects are to be found herein; and, whoever shall be pleased to favour me so far as to shew me my Errors; I shall stand infinitely obliged to them, being always very ready, and glad, to submit to superiour Judgments.*

As to Criticks, *I stand in no fear of them, for I have not Vanity enough to imagin that so mean a Performance will ever come under their Correction: And, if what I have delivered provoke some abler Pen to give a more full and perfect Account than what they will find here; it will be an intire Satisfaction to me, that I gave the Hint for promoting so noble an* Art.

N. B.

N. B. *I hope, the* Satyr *on the Abuse of* Musick, *at the End of this Book will not prove offensive to any; for as I did not write it with a Design to expose any particular Persons by Name; nor so much as pointed at any One whom it may affect; so if any should cavil at it, they are hereby desired to observe, that they are not therein included.*

The Reader is desired to observe the following

ERRATA.

Page 6. Line 10. after *not*, read *to*. P. 11. L. 16. after *has* read *a*. P. 31. L. 6. for 8. read 7. P. 49. in the last Line but One, for *makes*, read *make*. P. 50. L. 6. for *first*, read *fifth*.

Observe also, wherever you see the Word *Bass*, to read *Base*, excepting the 4th Line of the 39th Page, where it is spelt right.

A Philosophical Essay ON MUSICK, &c.

Of the Formation *of* Matter, *by* Nature.

HEN a Man fits himself seriously down upon the Chair of *Thought*, and duly reflects on the exact Uniformity that *Nature* has wrought, in her moulding the *human System* out of a Lump of *Earth*; and considers also, the wonderful Harmony there is in the Composition of each Member thereof, acting according to its respective *Office* or *Function*; in such a Manner as alone (besides the meer *Form* of *Humanity*,) distinguishes him from all other inferior Beings. He cannot but conclude, that there is Nothing, whatever, though ne'er so mean

B and

and unintelligible upon the Superfices, but what is capable, by some Method or other, of being reduced into a regular *Form* or *Order*. For Instance, What can any One think (who is a Stranger to the Experiment) of *the* Product of the industrious *Silk-Worm*; that it should by the Help of a little Art, yield Apparel gay enough for the noblest Courts? The laborious *Bee*, in forming the *Honey-Comb*, than which, what is in Art more exquisite? To omit a great many others, for Brevity's Sake, *Nature* has been so extraordinary liberal in distributing her Favours, (which visibly demonstrates an *invisible Hand* in all her Works) that she has indulged every Sense with Variety enough for every One's Palate: But there is One, which is feasted in a different Manner from the rest; and that is, the Sense of *Hearing*; for whatsoever is an Object of the *Eye*, affects also the *Touch*, the *Smell*, and the *Taste*, *Sound* alone being proper to the *Ear* only, which has its full Glutt with the others, in the infinite Variety that it is regaled with, by the beautiful Decorum of *Musical Cadences*; by which *Sound* (though it be not *Matter*, considered simply as such, but only a Production of *Matter*, by agitating the Air; which, when it is put into a convulsive Motion, strikes violently against the *Drum* of the *Ear*.) is regulated, and communicated in several Degrees; by either *Rising*, or *Falling*, according to the *Organ* thro' which it is conveyed. *First*, Through the *Organs* of *Speech*; as the *Wind-Pipe*, under the Government of the *Lungs*, is either extended or contracted in singing; which is effected by the various Emissions of *Breath*, in a gradual Progression, or by *Skips* from any one *Sound*, to what Distance you please. *Secondly*, Through that noble *Organ* the *Trumpet*; which, though it be not capable of *Extension*, yet is it under the same Discipline, and made obedient to the *Lungs*; and that in a diffe-

Marginalia:
By Art.
Omnipotence, the original Source from which, all Things have their Birth
What Sound is, and how communicated.
By the Organs of Speech, &c.

different Manner from the *Haut-boy*, *Flute*, &c. But my Design being to treat of the *Voice* only, I shall forbear enlarging on what is not so Material, and keep to my proper Subject.

A Regulation *from a* Plurality *of* Sounds.

OUR Business here, is not to consider so much what *Sound* is in its Essence, as in its Regulation; which consists of a Plurality of *Musical Sounds*, it being their Property to amuse the *Ear* with an agreeable Harmony: *Nature* having confined the Quality of their Number in their Progression, to a certain Period; whether this Limitation is owing to the different Qualities of *Atoms*, or to the Contrivance of the *Organs* of *Hearing*, or any other Cause; I shall leave to the Determination of much abler Heads, whenever they shall deem it worthy their Enquiry. It is sufficient here, to say, that there are but Seven different Degrees of Sound; *The Number of Sounds.* for when we rise to an *Eighth*, (begin where we will) it bears the same Likeness or Resemblance as the *First*: Just the same as when a Man Views the Mould and all the Features of his Face in a Looking-Glass. These Seven different *Sounds* or *Tones* are capable, some, of *Extension*; others, of *Contraction*, and Three of them, *Their Quality.* of both: Which they are, I shall shew in its proper Place. I am to observe here, that, as in the Art of *Astronomy*, &c. all *Lines* and *Circles* in the *Heavens* are Imaginary; so are *Sounds*: And as the former cannot *A Center absolutely necessary.* be practised without fixing a certain *Point* in the *Constellations*; so neither can *Musick* without a *Basis*. As to *Mathematicians*, they have more than an imaginary Point; but *Musicians* have nothing but what is so: Yet their *Art* is as practicable as the former; for they *Altogether Imaginary, yet not Impracticable.* fix a *Point* where they please; whereas, the others have one

one already fixed to their Hands, from which they cannot vary. And as *Muſicians,* all over *Europe,* and many other Places, mutually correſpond in this one Article; ſo they all agree in their *Ideas*; by making one particular *Tone* the *Standard* of their Performances, in fixing a certain *Pitch,* as they call it, which is as duly obſerved, by them all, as the *Axle-Tree* of a *Coach,* or *Cart*; or the *Standard* of *Weights* and *Meaſures.* But then, this is only for the convenience of Compoſers of *Muſick*; who are confined to dance, as it were, in a *Circle*; by limiting their *Vocal Muſick* to the Compaſs of the *Voices* which they compoſe for, there being ſeveral kinds of *Voices*; of which, we commonly reckon Four, *viz.* a *Baſe,* (which is the deepeſt) a *Tenor,* a *Contra-Tenor,* and a *Treble*; which laſt is the uppermoſt of all: Otherwiſe, upon Occaſion, it is wholly indifferent (eſpecially in ſinging) where a ſingle *Voice* takes its *Pitch,* ſo it obligeth it not to ſtretch too wide above, or below its natural Compaſs: But then, it is to be obſerved, that no *Inſtrument* is engaged with it; otherwiſe, the *Voice* or *Inſtrument* muſt give Way; for as regular *Tones* have a particular Relation to each other, where two or more are joyned together; ſo, where *Voices* or *Inſtruments,* or both, are performing together in Conſort, they muſt all move upon the ſame *Baſis,* or there can be no *Harmony,* but a confuſed Jumble of diſturbed *Atoms,* irregularly Jingling, very diſagreeably upon the *Ear-drum*; which is, what we call *Diſcords,* from their diſagreeing with one another.

Different Kinds of Voices.

Of the Relation of different Sounds, joyned together upon the ſame Baſis.

Of the ſeven Degrees of *Sound* before-mentioned, we muſt now ſuppoſe an *Eighth* or *Octave* to the *Sound* given; which, as I told you, bears its Reſemblance or Likeneſs; for without the *Octave,* they are not Perfect: becauſe, as aforeſaid, they depend upon a fixed *Point* or *Baſis,* from which we are to reckon them. And here
we

we are to confider, that as *Sounds* (as I have already obferved) affect only the *Ear*; fo have we nothing elfe to meafure them by, for that very Reafon. And as we are obliged to have recourfe to a given *Sound*; fo muft we fubmit to, and follow the Rules which *Nature* has made abfolute, having difpofed thefe feven Degrees of *Sound* in fuch a Manner as has made them capable of fo mathematical a Regulation, that *Mufick* is included among the *Liberal Sciences*, being one of the Seven, containing both *Number*, *Meafure* and *Proportion*. *Number*, in the different Lengths of continuing any of thofe *Sounds*; which Lengths are expreffed by as many different *Characters*. *Meafure*, in the dividing of thofe Lengths fpecified by fuch *Characters*, into fo many equal Parts, by the *Eye*, as well as the Diftance from one *Sound* to another, by the *Ear*. This is what may be called *Proportion* too; but there is another Kind of *Proportion*, which confifts in the different Divifions of *Parts* in *Songs* and *Tunes* of a different *Stamp*; all which, we fhall fpeak to, in their due Order, hereafter.

To be meafured by the Ear only.

Lengths of Sounds.

Meafured.

Several Kinds of Meafure.

We muft now proceed to affix Names to thefe feveral *Tones*, as being neceffary for their Diftinction; without which, we fhall be as far to feek as ever; there being no diftinguifhing any Thing, but by calling it by fome Name or other. The Names they are called by are the firft feven Letters in the *Alphabet*; which ftand in the *Kalendar*, to denote the Seven Days of the *Week*, thus, A, B, C, D, E, F, G; Any other Names might be given them, fo the Number Seven be obferved; *Mufick* not being confined to any particular *Words* or *Letters*; but you will fee the Reafon of applying the prefent Names to them, when I come to fpeak of them again. You may alfo, here perceive, that as every *Eighth* is the fame in Nature of

The Name of each Sound.

Sound

(6)

Sound,; fo, as we proceed higher, we muft confequently, call the *Ninth* by the fame Name as the *Second*; the *Tenth*, as the *Third*, &c. 'till we come to the *Fifteenth*; and fo on, as far as *Mufick* is practicable.

But e'er I proceed any farther upon this Head, I think it neceffary, as thefe feven Degrees of *Sound* depend, as I faid before, upon a fixed *Point* or *Bafis*, from which we are to reckon them; to examin the due Diftance of each, from the faid *Point* or *Sound* given.

Their Diſtances from their proper Bafis. What I mean by the Diftance of each, is not be underftood fimply, of the *Firft*, One Degree; the *Second* Two, and the like; for you may remember, I told you, (*Pag.* 3.) that the feven *Sounds* were capable, fome of them, of being extended, others contracted; and Three of them, of both *Extenfion* and *Contraction*; which they are, I come now to fhew.

How extended and contracted. By *Extenfion*, is meant, when a *Sound* rifeth from its natural Situation, half the Diftance (which is called a *Semitone*, or *Halftone*) between that and the next above it; and *Contraction*, when it falleth in the fame Proportion towards the *Sound* below it; fuch Paffages being very frequent, both in *Vocal* and *Inftrumental Mufick*, and are what we call *artificial*, or *chromatick Sounds*.

The Quality of a Third to the Sound given. The *Sound* given is called the *Key* to the reft, whofe *Third* (which is the *Second* above it, the *Key* itſelf being always included as the *Firft*) muft be either a *Major*, or a *Minor*; that is, a whole *Tone* or a *Semitone* to its *Second*; the firft of which is capable only of *Contraction*, the *Fourth*, which is the next above it, rendring it incapable of what we here call *Extenfion*; a *Semitone* being the minuteft Diftance from one *Sound* to another.

Now, with the *major Third*, the *major Sixth*, is naturally required; and alfo the *major Seventh*, the *Second*, *Fourth*, and *Fifth* being always the fame Diftance from the

the *Key* in the *Major* as in the *minor Third*; that is to say, the *greater* or *lesser Third*. Where, note by the Way, that the *Second* is always a whole *Tone* from the *Key*, and the *Fifth*, always the same Distance from the *Fourth*. By all which, you may readily perceive that as the *Fourth* under the (give me leave to call it) *Administration* of the *major Third*, is but a *Semitone* to the same; so is the *Eighth* the same Distance from the *major Seventh*; there being two *Semitones* between the Sound given and its *Octave*. Now, as the *Fourth* and *Eighth* are but *Semitones* to those immediately below them; they cannot be contracted for the Reasons abovesaid; nor can the *Third* or *Seventh* be extended, for the same Reason; those *Sounds* only which are whole *Tones* both to those above and below them, being capable of both *Extension* and *Contraction*; which are the *Second, Fifth* and *Sixth*. By the same Rule, when the *Third* to the *Key* is but a *Semitone* to its *Second*; i. e. the *Minor* or *Lesser Third*; there the *Third* and *Sixth* bear the same Proportion as the *Fourth* and *Eighth* in the former; the *Second* and *Fifth*, the same as the *Third* and *Seventh*; and the *Fourth, Seventh*, and *Eighth*, the same as the *Second, Fifth*, and *Sixth*. From all which, it appears, that as there are Two of the Seven Degrees of Sound but *Semitones*, as beforehinted; so is the Distance of the *Octave*, by the *Rule* of *Proportion*, but six whole *Tones* from the supposed *Sound* given, which must of Course contain double the Number of *Semitones*, which divide the eight *Sounds* into twelve equal Parts, as you will better understand hereafter.

Its Predominancy.

The

The different Effects of Sound.

NOW, it is the property of *Sound* in general, to prove either pleasing or offensive; as in the Case of a strong sudden Clap of *Thunder*; nay, if it be but a small Report of that diminutive Instrument of Fate, called a *Pocket-Pistol*, coming with an unexpected Salutation upon the *Ear:* I need not tell you, what daily Experience shews, into what a Disorder it puts a Man at that Instant, setting the Nerves a Trembling throughout the whole *human Fabrick*. And as it is so in confused *Sounds*, so is it, in some Measure in those which are, in their own Nature regular, when they are irregularly managed; for you may remember what I said, *(Page* 4.) of *Discords*, or the disagreeing of *Sounds*; where several are improperly joyned together, let them be either *Discords* or *Concords*, the latter of which being termed so, as being their Property to please the *Ear* (or rather, the *Fancy*) when managed judiciously; otherwise, a nice *Ear* will be very much offended, false *Concords* not being allowed in *Musick*, any more than in *Grammar*.

A great Mistake in modern Musicians.

AND here I hope I shall not incur the Displeasure of any, if I crave leave to throw in an Objection against the common Notions of most of (if not all) our modern *Musicians*, who look upon the *Fourth* as a *Discord*, the Definition of a *Discord* being a *Sound* which is ungrateful to the *Ear*; and whether the *Fourth* be so or not, the *Ear* must be the Judge: And I never yet heard any one pretend that it is disagreeable; nay, rather the contrary, for that the *Fourth* is concern'd in the Resolution of all *Cadences*; it being directly contrary to

the

the Nature of *Musick* to close with any Sound that's disagreeable: Wherefore, 'till I can see some satisfactory Reason to the contrary; I hope I may, without a Breach of Modesty, assume the Liberty of ranging the *Fourth* in the Number of *Concords*; which are the *Third*, (major or *minor*) the *Fourth*, (perfect) the *Fifth*, (perfect) the *Sixth* (major or *minor*) and the *Eighth*: So that the *Concords* are (not Four only, but) Five in Number, *viz.* the *Third*, *Fourth*, *Fifth*, *Sixth* and *Eighth*; the *Second* and *Seventh* only, being properly termed *Discords*, from their jangling with the *Basis*. And even these, when artfully introduced, yield a most agreeable *Harmony*, as well as some others; which may not be improperly termed *Discords*, although it be the *Third*, *Fourth*, *Fifth* or *Sixth*, &c. when they are occasionally extended or contracted, according to their Capacity. *The Number of Concords and Discords.*

It may perhaps, be here expected, that as I have given the Definition of *Concords* and *Discords*; so that I should also give a Reason why such and such *Cords*, as the *Second* and *Seventh* should be *Discords*, any more than the others, which are called *Concords*? That is, what is the natural Cause thereof? (tho' it be not at all material to give an Answer, if one could) The only Satisfaction I can give such curious Enquirers, next referring them back to *pag.* 5. is, that it may probably be; because the *Second* being but one Degree from its *Basis*, may create such a Disagreement from its lying so near to its *Center*; for where there is any Appearance of Uneasiness, the closer the *Object* presses, the greater will the Grievance be; from whence, naturally ariseth the following *Paradox*, viz. *The nearer they meet, the farther they are asunder*; for it is not good to be too Familiar. What has been said of the *Second*, may be as applicable to the *Seventh*, as bearing the same Proportion. *A curious Question considered.*

C *In*

In what Manner the Concords *are sometimes* Discords. *The* Fifth *a* Perfect Concord, *and why so called. The* Harmony *of* Sounds *comprized in* Three *only.*

IT sometimes happens, that the *Third*, tho' naturally a *Concord*, becomes a *Discord*, by being joyned with the *Fourth*: The *Fourth* is also a *Discord*, when joyned with the *Fifth*; the *Fifth* also, (tho' it is called a perfect *Concord*, from the Perfection of its Quality, the *Harmony* of *Sounds* being imperfect without it; for no more than Three can be joyned together without the Encroachment of a *Discord*; and as *concording Sounds* are limited to Three only, *viz.* the *Sound* given, the *Third* and the *Fifth*; so the Latter, being the greatest Distance between the given *Sound* and the *Octave*, and subject to no *Extension* or *Contraction*, (as it relates to the *Base*, in its natural *Situation*) communicates *Perfection* to that which wou'd otherwise, be very imperfect, and) is a *Discord*, when joyned with the *Sixth*: The *Sixth* is also a *Discord*, when joyned with the *Seventh*: But this latter seldom happens.

The Reason that these *Concords* we are speaking of become *Discords* is, that in the aforesaid Conjunction, they are *Seconds* to each other; yet still-remain *Concords* to the *Base*; from all which, *natural Reason* dictates, that there is no possibility of adding a fourth *Sound* in Conjunction with three others of any Kind; but that one or the other, must consequently become a *Discord*. If the *Eighth* be supposed, it is no *Objection*; for, being the same with the *First*, it makes no Alteration, and therefore is not a fourth *Sound*, all *Eighths* being the same: For as the *Eighth* is to the *First*, so is the *Tenth* to the *Third*, the *Twelfth* to the *Fifth*, &c.

The Reason why the Third and Fifth are called Common Cords.

BUT some will be apt to ask, (and with very good Reason) why the *Third* and *Fifth* are mentioned particularly, apart from the other *Concords*? To which, it may be answered, that all *Cadences* Center in those *Cords*; for which Reason they are called *Common-Cords*, as being nearest to the *Base*; wherefore it is unnatural to close with either the *Third* and *Sixth*, or the *Fourth* and *Sixth*; which are all that can be supposed.

Again, the *Third* may become a *Discord* to the *Base* by Way of *Contraction*, according to what I observed, (*pag. 9.*) but then it must be the *major Third* which is proposed; and that is when it descends half a *Tone*, and the *Base* at the same Time ascends as much; which is but the Quantity of a *Second*; altho' it has different Effect upon the *Ear*, according as it is introduced by the *Sounds* foregoing, a just Decorum being to be observed in composing of *Musick*, as well as in making an eloquent Speech, &c. with the choicest Flowers of *Rhetorick*; the subject of the *Air* requiring to be kept up as nicely as the Rules of *Grammar*; without which, tho' it may relish tollerably well with an undiscerning Palate; yet, to a judicious One it will be very unsavory: For it would be but an unpleasant Entertainment to a fine *Orator* to hear any Man talk, or write, downright Nonsense; though some others may be well enough pleased with it.

The *Fourth* may become a *Discord* to the *Base* two Ways; *First*, by extending the *Base* in the same Manner as aforesaid; which is the Quantity of a *major Third*, but yet is a *Discord*, and may be called an *imperfect Fourth*; but is seldom used. *Secondly*, it becomes a *Discord*, when it extends itself, while the *Bass* keeps its proper Place, and is called the *Tritone*, or *greater Fourth*, being three whole *Tones* from the *Bass*, which is just half the Distance between the *Bass* and the *Octave*.

The *Fifth* also, may two ways, become a *Discord* to the *Bass*; the First is, when the *Bass* ascends half a *Tone*, and is called the *Semidiapente* or *imperfect Fifth*, bearing the same Proportion as the *Tritone*. Secondly, It becomes a *Discord* when it extends itself and has the Quantity of a *minor Sixth*; bearing the same Proportion as the *imperfect Fourth*, and is as seldom used.

The *Sixth* is sometimes a *Discord* to the *Base*, by Way of *Extension*, and has the same Proportion as the *Third*, before spoken of; both which, are very rarely used.

Note, That these *Cords* are not always confined to joyn with the *Base*, but may happen as well among the other Parts. The Reason that I appropriate them to the *Base* is, because, as it is the Ground-Work of all *Musick*, it makes it so much the more intelligible to those that are, as yet, unexperienced.

Sometimes the *Second*, by extending it self, has the Quantity of a *Third Minor*; but then it still remains a *Discord*. The *Seventh* also, by descending half a *Tone*, while the *Base* extends itself, has the Quantity of a *major Sixth*; but, like the *Second*, still continues a *Discord*.

The *Eighth*, on some extraordinary Occasions, becomes a *Discord*; and that is, when the *Base* extends it self, which is the Quantity of a *major Seventh*: And also, when the *Eighth* descends half a *Tone*, (the *Base* keeping its proper Place) it has the same Proportion: But this is as rare, almost, as *Frost* in *June*.

Musick

(13)

Musick extraordinary comprehensive. In what Manner.

THE *Bearings* of all these *Discords*, and *Concords*, in their *Turns*, are of excellent *Signification*, as well as infinite in *Variation*; and we may truly say, that *Musick* itself, includes in some Measure, the whole seven *Literal-Arts*: For there is not any *Sentence* in *Speech*, but what is to be expressed in *Musick* by the help of some *Cadence* answerable to each *Sentence*; for as there are different Kinds of *Sentences*; or, to speak more intelligibly, different *Matter* for *Expression*, according to the *Subject* spoken of; so are there as many different *Cadences*, directly answering them all, alluding to the several *Points* or *Stops*, in *Writing*: And as its *Scope* is infinite; so must its *Numbers* also be, with Respect to its infinite *Variation*. *Chromatick Musick* may be said to be *Geometrical*, by extending and contracting of *Sounds*, (such as those *Discords* just now spoken of) from their natural Situation, *&c*. The seven plain Degrees of *Sound*, may be said to bear an Allusion to the seven *Planets*, taking the *Sun* for the *Center* or *Basis*; and then the *Earth* comes in for its Share, to make up an *Eighth*; as also, the dividing the eight *Sounds* into twelve Degrees, alludes to the twelve *Constellations* of the *Zodiack*. Here is a very great *Mistery*, which confounds all our *Philosophy*; and which *Time* will hardly, I believe, ever account for. Besides all this, it expresseth all the different Passions of Mankind, and not only so; but by the Force of its most prevailing Charms, it wonderfully affects them too; and to such a Degree, that *Musick* may be justly called (for which I have (*) something more than *Human Authority*) an enchanting *Art*; by sometimes giving

Its surprising Effects.

(*) *See,* 1 Sam. 16, 23.

giving a Loose too ; and at others, by bridling our unruly Inclinations, according to the Subject which is composed, and the interweaving of the different Parts moving together in *Harmony* ; one while inclining the Minds of People to deliver themselves up to *sensual Pleasures*, by indulging the insatiable *carnal Appetite*, which knows no Limits ; and at other Times, when rightly applied, it affords such internal Comfort to them as disengages their Thoughts from all earthly Enjoyments, and disposes the Soul to look with earnest Attention, on the only Object of its true Felicity, the *Beatifick-Vision*. This, and a great deal more may be said, to display its Excellencies ; although there are some of so unhappy a Cast, that instead of being delighted with it, they utterly contemn it ; notwithstanding its eternal Duration in the *Realms of Bliss*. But, to return to the Thread of my Subject,

As I have given you a brief Account of the Names commonly applied to these seven Degrees of *Sound*, with their Distances from the *Key* or *Basis* ; together with the natural Capacity of each : So I now suppose it high Time, to give a Specimen of the *Stations* and *Characters* by which they are distinguished, both as to their *Number*, *Measure* and *Proportion*, &c. as I formerly promised. For,

As the Progression of *Sounds*, naturally forms an *Idea* in the *Imagination* of something that ascends one Way, and descends the other ; so are we obliged to form a *Scheme*, that may represent such *Ideas* to the *Eye*, in Order to a right Understanding of them. Wherefore, I shall proceed in as familiar a Way as I can, and lay down the Rules in such a Manner, as I hope, will rather engage the Attention of my Readers, than perplex them with such Intricacies as may be apt to confound them, and prove more puzzling than edifying.

To

To which End, I shall begin with the *Characters* or *Notes*, by which the Lengths of *Sounds* are measured; for as Time ought to be first consulted in every Thing we undertake; so I think, we ought to take it before us here; and when once that is accounted for, we shall see more clearly, and consequently, understand more at large what we are going upon.

Now, as *Motion* is the Mother of *Time*, so is *Time* the *Measurer* thereof; and as we cannot account for *Motion*, without a *Regulation*; (as it is in *Years, Months, Seasons,* &c.) so, neither can we account for *Musick*, without the Assistance of *Time*; by which, it also becomes a *Regulator* or *Measurer* of that; there being nothing to be done without this *old Acquaintance*. Therefore, the *Notes* or *Characters* aforementioned, are of different Species, on Purpose to denote the different *Lengths* of *Sounds*; otherwise, one alone would have been sufficient.

The Number of the Notes *used in* Musick. *Their* Measure *and* Proportion.

OF these *Notes*, there are but six commonly used; the longest of which is called a *Semibreve*, or half the Measure of a *Breve*, which latter, is now very rare to be met with but in *Church-Musick*; tho' formerly it was very much in Use, as well as two other *Notes*, which are also now, wholly laid aside, and therefore not pertinent to insert here. It is enough to say, that as the *Semibreve* was once the shortest Note but one, in use; it is now the longest, from which all the other *Notes* (which have been since introduced) have their *Measure*: Their *Proportion* being thus, *viz.* As *Two* are to *One*, so are *Four* to *Two*; *Eight* to *Four*; *Sixteen* to *Eight*; and *Thirty Two* to *Sixteen*: Each of which *Notes* is various in its *Length*, i. e. not in all

Airs

(16)

Airs alike, according to the *Air* which is composed, (some Movements being slow, and others brisk, in conformity to the various Subjects in *Musick*,) but are nevertheless, at all Times, to take their *Dimensions* from the *Semibreve*, in such Movements as it is supposed to be engaged in, as being the *Master-Note*, or *Grand Mover*, of the whole Body ; to which, they must all be subservient, as the Motions of the lower *Orbs* are to the *Primum Mobile*.

The *Breve*, (if it should at any Time fall in your Way) is marked thus, ⌶ which I insert, because several, who practise Singing, although they do not perform in any of our *Choirs*, yet take much Delight (as it is to be wish'd all People did) in *Church-Musick*.

The *Semibreve* is divided into *Two* and *Thirty Parts*, *Sixteen*, *Eight*, *Four* or *Two*. Its Mark is this, ◯

The Name of each Note.   The first *Note* that shews these Divisions, is called a *Minim* ; marked like the *Semibreve*, and is distinguished from it by the Addition of a Tail, thus ; 𝄐 which being but half the Length of the *Semibreve*, divides it into two equal Parts.

The Second is called a *Crotchet* ; marked like the *Minim* with the Head filled up, thus ; 𝄑 which being but half the Length of the *Minim*, divides the *Semibreve* into *Four* Parts.

The Third is called a *Quaver* ; marked like the *Crotchet*, and is distinguished from it, by the Tail's being turned up again, thus ; 𝄒 which being but half the Length of the *Crotchet*, divides the *Semibreve* into *Eight* Parts.

The

(17)

The Fourth is called a *Semiquaver*; which being but half the Length of the *Quaver*, has its Tail turned up with a double Stroke, thus; and divides the *Semibreve* into *Sixteen* Parts.

The Fifth, and Last, is called a *Demifemiquaver* or *Demiquaver*; which being but half the Length of the *Semiquaver*, has its Tail turned up with a tripple Stroke, thus; and divides the *Semibreve* into *Two* and *Thirty* Parts. The following *Scheme* will give you the whole at one View.

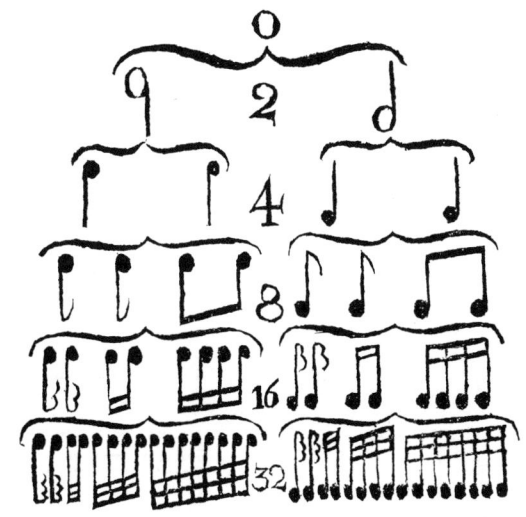

Here you see all the Species of *Quavers* differently marked, and also in different Positions; some single, and the rest tied together; some with their Heads lying upward, and the others with their Heads downward. The Reason for the first of which is, that, as there are

D some-

sometimes several *Notes* to be sung in one *Vowel*; (which are called *Diminutions* or *Divisions*) they are tied together to save the Trouble of Writing each *Note* singly, by itself; which otherwise wou'd take up more Time in penning them down; and would be also, more difficult for the *Eye*: This Way of tying them, shewing their *Measure*, altogether the same as if they were single; for, you see that the *Quavers*, instead of the Stroke to their Tails, are tied with one Stroke through Two and sometimes more of them. The *Semiquavers* also, instead of a double Stroke, have two Ties, and the *Demiquavers* Three. The Reason of turning their Heads differently, is because the Situation of the *Notes* being represented upon a certain Number of *Lines*, with their intermediate *Spaces*; according as they happen to lie, either higher or lower; so they are writ down in a different Manner, to prevent their interfering with one another: For the better explaining of which, I shall here give you a *Sample*.

Here you see the convenience of it, there being nothing more plain than *occular Demonstration*. You see also, the Measure of the *Semibreve* in each *Staff* or Number of *Lines*, represented by a *Minim*, a *Crotchet* and two *Quavers*.

For

For the better underſtanding of *Time* or *Meaſure*, it is to be conſidered, that as there are *Cadences*, (as I obſerved *pag.* 13.) anſwerable to all Manner of *Sentences*, &c. So is there an *Emphaſis* or *Accent*, that begins each *Meaſure* ; to which a *Beat* with the *Hand* or *Foot*, is a very neceſſary Aſſiſtant to a *Learner* ; tho' ſuch as have made any conſiderable Progreſs in *Muſick*, do it by the Force of Imagination. And for the better help thereof, (eſpecially in ſinging or playing in *Conſort*) there is a *Bar* always placed before each *Note* that is to be beat upon, which *Bar* runs thro' all the *Lines* ; as you may ſee in the late *Example :* And when you come half through each *Bar* or *Meaſure* of *Time*, (they being all equal) the *Hand* or *Foot*, muſt be lifted up again ; as at the ſecond *Minim*, the third *Crotchet*, the fifth *Quaver*, &c. according as the *Meaſures* are divided ; for although the Quantity of each is the ſame; yet their Variations are many, as I have hinted before ; and which, I am going to explain more fully.

The Method of ſquaring Time.

The Proportion *of different* Meaſures. *Of* Common-Time. *The Number of* Moods *uſed therein.*

THERE are ſeveral other *Characters* called *Moods*, by which, (as I told you, *pag.* 5.) the different Diviſions of *Parts* or *Meaſures*, in *Songs* and *Tunes* of a different *Stamp*, are diſtinguiſhed. Of theſe, there are twelve Sorts in Uſe ; but none of them confined to keep the ſame Pace in each different *Mood* in all *Tunes*, unleſs it be in what we call *Common-Time*, (from the equal Diviſions of its *Meaſures*, as two *Minims*, four *Crotchets*, eight *Quavers*, &c.) for which there are four *Moods*. The Reaſon that there are ſo many, is becauſe all *Tunes* (as I ſaid above) do not keep the ſame Pace, though the

the *Measures* are equally divided. The Sign of the first of these *Moods* is this ; C which denotes the slowest *Movement*, and is always counted by *Crotchets*, (as all the *Common Moods* are) the *Quavers* being, rather too minute for the Fancy to engage in. In this *Mood*, the *Crotchets* may be measured by the beating of the lively *Pulse* ; but not to be depended on for a Regularity, though the Body be in never so good Order.

The *Sign* of the second *Mood* in *Common-Time* is the same as the first, with this Difference only, *viz.* the drawing a *Bar* through it, thus ; ₵ which denotes the *Movement* to be somewhat faster than the former.

In the third Sort of *Common-Time*, the *Sign* of the *Mood* is reversed, thus ; ₱ which is the quickest of all ; the *Crotchets* being counted as fast as the regular Motions of a *Watch*.

Thus you see, what I said before (*pag.* 15.) that *Notes* of the same Species are various in their *Lengths*, according to the Subject of the *Air* which is composed.

The fourth *Mood* in *Common-Time* has but two *Crotchets*, to a *Measure*, for which Reason it is marked thus ; $\frac{2}{4}$ that is, two *Crotchets* from four. This is commonly sung or play'd pretty quick ; but the Reason for making Use of such a *Mood* as this, I do not well understand, since four *Crotchets* may be as well made use of as two : But, because you will often find it ; I thought it Necessary to give you the meaning of this as well as of the others.

Of

Of Triple-Time. *The different* Moods *used therein.*

THE other *Moods*, which are eight in Number, are proper to what we call *Tripple-Time*, and divide the *Measures* into three equal Parts; or sometimes but two; and at others into four; *i. e.* three Times *One*; (by *Minims*, *Crotchets* or *Quavers*) three Times *Three*; (by *Crotchets* or *Quavers*) two times *Three*; (by *Crotchets* or *Quavers*) and four Times *Three*; (by *Quavers*) for this *Tripple-Time* has been so minced and muffled, that its true Face is now hardly discernable; and is more apt to provoke a *Learner* to throw by his *Book* with Contempt, than encourage him to proceed in what his Inclinations may be most bent upon. And, in this Particular, there has been a very great Deficiency in many, who profess themselves to be *Teachers* of *Musick*, who (either through Laziness or Ignorance being unable to give a true Definition of what they ought to be most careful in) leave their *Pupils* as Ignorant as themselves: For it is certain, that *Musick* can never be thoroughly understood without our being Masters of *Time*, in all its *Branches*. Wherefore, that I may not leave my Readers in the Dark; I shall give them a due Account of it, and clear up all the seeming Difficulties that appear as so many *Stumbling-Blocks* in the Progress of this *Science*.

The first of these *Tripple-Movements* is measured by three *Minims*, and is marked thus; $\frac{3}{2}$ that is, three *Minims* to two, which is borrowing half a *Measure* from the *Common-Moods*, by the Addition of a *Minim*. These are beat, *Two* with the *Hand* down, and *One* with it up. Those *Measures* that are divided by *Crotchets* in this *Mood*, are to be beat, *Four* down and *Two* up;

if

if *Quavers*, then *Eight* and *Four*, as you may readily conceive, by the Rule of Proportion. I think it Necessary also, to inform you, that *Quavers* are (unless upon some extraordinary Occasion) the minutest *Notes* used in this *Mood*: Nor is the *Semibreve* here excluded; for you will often meet with the *Semibreve* and a *Minim* in some of these *Measures*; and sometimes the *Semibreve* only; which has then, a small *Point* or *Dot* added to it, thus; ⌐ which adds to it, half its former Quantity, being called a *pointed Semibreve*. The same is to be understood of any of the other *Notes*, when they have a *Point* placed before them; it being always on the Right-Hand Side of each.

The Second *Mood*, (which answers this) is measured by three *Crotchets*, marked thus; $\frac{3}{4}$ that is, three *Crotchets* from four; in which it differs from the other, no otherwise than in being measured by different *Notes*: For in the former *Mood*, *Minims* are sometimes, as fast as *Crotchets*; and in this, the *Crotchets* are often as slow as *Minims*. The only Rule that is to be given for the Length of *Notes* in this Case, is that where the Movement is *Slow*; they always write the Word *Slow* at the Beginning of each *Lesson*: Or at least, ought always so to do, the *Moods* in *Triple-Time* not at all denoting now, (though formerly they did) what is to be sung *Slow* or *Fast*, as they do in *Common-Time*. Those *Measures* that are divided by *Quavers* in this *Mood*, are to be beat the same as the *Crotchets* in the former: If *Semiquavers*, then the same as the *Quavers*; the *Semiquavers* being the minutest *Notes* used in this *Mood*. The *Ruling-Note* here, is a *Pointed-Minim*.

The third *Mood*, (which answers to the two former) is measured by three *Quavers*, marked thus; $\frac{3}{8}$ which is three *Quavers* from eight, (minute enough) and is exactly the same with the others: For in this *Mood*, the

the *Quavers* are sometimes, as slow as *Minims* are in the first. The *Measures* divided by *Semiquavers* in this *Mood*, are to be beat answerable to the two former; that is, *Four* and *Two*: If *Demiquavers*, then *Eight* and *Four*. I need not tell you that the latter are the minutest *Notes* in this *Mood*, because (as I have already signified to you) they are the shortest *Notes* used in *Musick*. The chief *Note* here, is a *pointed Crotchet*.

These are all the *Measures* that are, or can, I think, possibly be in *Triple-Time*, unless a new Species of *Notes* were invented: For *Semiquavers* are too minute to form a *Mood* in; because there is but one Degree of *Notes* beyond them, (it always requiring two) which are the *Demiquavers*. Sometimes indeed, in *instrumental Musick*; by Way of Embellishment, to express any Thing lofty, and the like, we shall meet with *Quavers* tied together with four Strokes, which are play'd but half the Length of the *Demiquavers*: But these are so rare to be met with in *vocal Musick*, that it is not worth while to give you a Specimen of them, the Imagination alone, being sufficiently able to furnish you with as perfect an *Idea* of them, as if you were to see them writ down. And if at any Time, you should meet with them; by making yourself perfect in what you have been here already informed of, you will be at no Manner of Loss in the Execution of them.

But before I leave this Head, I must not omit to give you some farther Account of this *Triple-Time*; for besides the *Measure* of three Times *One*, by *Minims*, *Crotchets* or *Quavers*; as I told you, (*pag.* 21.) and which I have given you a full Description of: I also told you, in the same Page, of measuring by Three Times *Three*, &c. by *Crotchets* or *Quavers*. And this is no more than trippling the *Mood* of $\frac{3}{4}$ and that of $\frac{3}{8}$: The first is nine *Crotchets*; which is barring in

three

three *Measures* together; for which they have this Mark $\frac{9}{4}$; and which we may call nine *Crotchets* to four. The Reason for this barring in three *Measures* together, I do not, indeed, disapprove of; because all *Songs* being writ in *Metre*, there is at least, a seeming Necessity for so doing: For in writing of *Verse*, there are the same Diversities of *Numbers* and *Measures*, &c. as there are in *Musick*: For which Reason, *Sound* ought to conform, in its *Measures*, to *Sense*: Wherefore, as in *Poetical-Numbers*, there are often *Measures* of three Times *Three*, in each *Line* or *Verse*; (as, (if you consider the *Accents* in each) you may perceive in the following *Distych*; in which, I shall put a *Dash* over each *Vowel* that carries an *Accent*, viz.

" if you wou'd knòw a Thing rèadily;
" Yòu must applỳ your self stèadily.)

accordingly (these *Numbers* being of a sprightly Cast, and ought consequently, to be pretty swift in their Motion) they bar in three *Measures* together; that they who sing or play, may beat but once in three of each: For to beat at every *Measure*, would eclipse the Sense of the *Poet*, by a Kind of *dancing* with the Hand or Foot, that is supposed to beat those *Measures*, and so balk the *Ear*, both Ways: For though it be a *dancing-Measure*; we are not therefore, by beating oftner than is requisite, to keep an unnecessary Rumbling, though these *Bars* will admit of three *Beats* in each. The *Notes* here, are beat *Six* down, and *Three* up; there being no *Quavers* made use of, but what follow (Now and Then one of them) after a *pointed-Crotchet*; or sometimes, preceeding it. To alot any one *Note* for a whole *Measure* in this *Mood* is not possible; the *pointed Semibreve* being the longest of any, which wants three *Crotchets* to make it good: 'Therefore, where there is in any of these *Measures*, but one *Note* supposed; they

put

put three *pointed Minims*, (which are equal to nine *Crotchets*) bound with *Arches* over their *Heads*, thus; which signifies that they are to be, all three continued as one *Note*.

But although this *Mood* of $\frac{9}{4}$ may be very reasonably allowed; yet, I can see no manner of Reason why the other spoken of, of $\frac{9}{8}$ (which is nine *Quavers* barred in together) should be made use of: Or if it be admitted, what Occasion there is for both? For, the *Measures* of the *Quavers* and the *Crotchets* are both equal in these two *Moods*, the latter moving as quick, in the *Mood* of $\frac{9}{4}$ as the *Quavers* in this *Mood* of $\frac{9}{8}$: But as you will meet with one, as often as the other; I thought my self under an indispensible Obligation to acquaint you with it. The *Measures* in this *Mood* (I hardly need to tell you) are beat, the same as in the *Mood* of $\frac{9}{4}$; *i. e.* Six down, and *Three* up: A whole *Measure* in one continued *Sound* being represented by three *Pointed-Crotchets*, thus;

Again, the *Measures* that are divided into two equal Parts, as in *pag.* 21. are specified by *Crotchets* or *Quavers*. The first is by doubling the *Mood* of $\frac{3}{4}$ and the latter, that of $\frac{3}{8}$ (two *Measures* being barred in together in each) For the former, they have this *Mark* $\frac{6}{4}$; which is six *Crotchets* to four, and which are beat *Three* down, and *Three* up; the *Quavers* in this *Mood* being introduced the same as in the *Mood* of $\frac{9}{4}$. When a whole *Measure*, in one continued *Sound* is met with here; it is represented by a *Pointed Semibreve* ☉. or (rather) two *Pointed Minims*, thus; as more aptly shew-

ing

ing the equal *Divisions* of *Parts*, which is much more natural. For the latter; that is, when the *Mood* $\frac{3}{4}$ is doubled, its *Sign* is this; $\frac{6}{8}$ that is, six *Quavers* from eight, and answers the same in Proportion, as the former: But then, I cannot perceive what Occasion there is for this *Mood*, any more than that of $\frac{2}{4}$ the *Crotchets* being in their Turns, as brisk as the *Quavers*. Sometimes they have *Semiquavers* in these *Measures*, which are beat *Six* down, and *Six* up; as also, *Quavers* in the *Mood* of $\frac{6}{4}$ but then, I think there is no Occasion for doubling of either of the *Moods*.

The eighth (and last) *Mood* in *Tripple-Time*, which divides the *Measures* into four Times *Three*, (as in *pag.* 21.) is barring in four of the *Measures* together in the *Mood* of $\frac{3}{8}$ represented by twelve *Quavers*, marked thus; $\frac{12}{8}$ which is twelve *Quavers* to eight. I will not be so Ill-natur'd, as to dispute the Reasonableness of this *Mood*, where it is aptly applied; which is in very swift *Movements*, as *Jiggs*, &c. but why it should be made use of in slow (sometimes, very slow) *Movements*, I cannot conceive; since the *Mood* of $\frac{3}{8}$ (which takes in but one of these four *Measures*) may do much better, especially for the convenience of *Scholars*; or rather, the *Mood* of $\frac{3}{4}$, or that of $\frac{3}{2}$; which barrs in three *Minims*, they seeming to me, to be much more Proper than *Quavers*, to denote slow *Movements*: For, if such a Method were put in Practise, there would be no manner of Occasion to write (at the beginning of *Lessons*) the *Italian* Words, *Adagio, Grave, Largo,* &c. (which are put before slow *Movements*) or *Allegro, Presto, Vivace,* &c. (which are applied to swift *Movements*: And which they do in all the *Moods* hitherto spoken of, without Exception) there being Variety sufficient in the different Species of the *Notes* themselves, to shew what *Movement* is slow, and what brisk; without

out putting our *Pupils*, or our felves, to the Trouble of learning Foreign Languages. A whole *Meafure* of one *Sound* in the aforefaid *Mood* of 12/8 may be reprefented by either a *Pointed Semibreve*, (which is the Quantity of twelve *Quavers*) two *Pointed Minims*, (which are the fame) or (more properly) four *Pointed Crotchets*, thus;

Sometimes you will meet with this *Mark*; which is commonly put for the *Mood* of ¾; but ought to be quite thrown afide, were it but for the Convenience of *Learners:* For I know not what Occafion there is for having two *Signs* to one *Mood*.

There is yet another Whim that fome People have got; which is to place a Figure of at the Beginning of moft, if not all their *Leffons* in *Tripple-Time*; a pretty Method enough to put a Mask over a Face that they (perhaps) Fancy too good for every Body to fee.

All the Moods *in* Triple-Time *reduced to one only.*

UPON the whole, out of all thefe eight *Moods* I have been fpeaking of, there is, in reality, but *One*: That which is fuppofed, may be either that of three *Minims* to a *Meafure*, or that of three *Crotchets*, or the *Mood* of three *Quavers*. The Reafon for the doubling and trippling of fome of which, I have already given; and the Reafons for the others, I cannot well underftand: But muft Neverthelefs, bear an implicit Faith in me, that they have a meanning in them,

E 2 perti-

(28)

pertinent enough, though I want the Capacity of finding it out ; and if any, can inform me, of the Significancy of what appears to me, to be Infignificant: I fhall readily recant my Error, and own my felf highly obliged to them, for fetting me to rights, in a Matter that I am, as yet, an entire Stranger to.

A *Scheme* of all thefe *Moods*, will reprefent it felf to the *Reader*, in the following View.

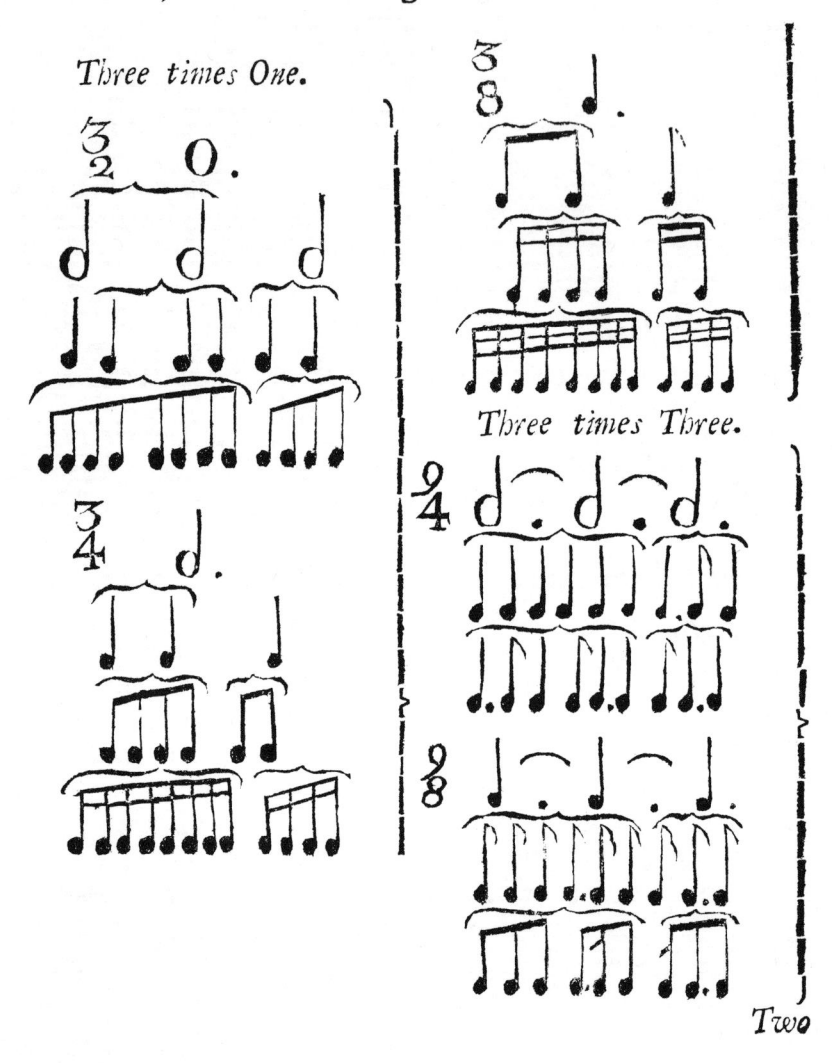

Three times One.

Three times Three.

Two

(29)

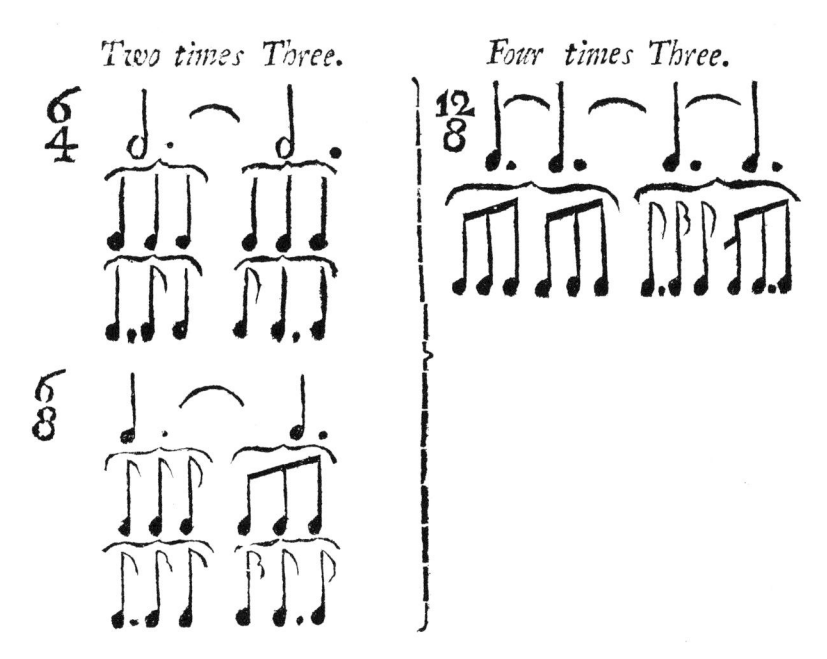

Two times Three.   *Four times Three.*

I have once, (and but once) seen in a very ingenious Author, the *Mood* of $\frac{3}{2}$ doubled; which barrs in six *Minims*: Three whereof, to be beat with the *Hand* down, and three up; marked thus; $\frac{6}{2}$ that is, six *Minims* to two; and also another *Mood*, consisting of no more than six *Semiquavers*, barred in Three and Three, like the former, marked thus; $\frac{6}{16}$ that is, six *Semiquavers* from sixteen. Yet, notwithstanding the Sanction which a great Name may give to a Thing that has nothing else to countenance it, I must leave my *Readers* to judge, by what I have already delivered, what Occasion there may be for the Use of two such *Moods*, unless it be to save a Composer the Trouble of making more *Barrs* than what he may (perhaps) think he has Occasion for, in the first: And to shew himself singular in the last, if not in both; which is all I need to

say

say farther upon this Head: Only I shall observe, that, before *Musick* was come to the Perfection it is now arrived at, there were no *Barrs* in Use; and if People continue to grow Whimsick-all, (as who knows what extraordinary Effects may be produced from the late *Tripple-Conjunction*) I don't know, but that in a little Time, we shall have no more Occasion for them; tho' at present, we can't do without 'em.

I come, in the next Place, to shew you the Situation of the *Sounds* before spoken of, according to what I told you, *(pag.* 14.*)* by forming a *Scheme,* in Order to a right Understanding of their Distances, &c. which is represented on a *Staff* of Five *Lines,* with their intermediate *Spaces*; as mentioned, *(pag.* 18.) not that such a Number is sufficient to shew the whole Compass of *Musick,* but for the ease of the Sight; because, if there were to be more, the *Eye* could not so readily catch them: And where there is Occasion to proceed, either above or below each *Staff*; so they make use of additional *Lines*; struck just through, or underneath the *Head* of each of the *Notes* before-mentioned, according as they shall happen to lie, as you may perceive, by turning back, to *pag.* 18. which I shall explain more fully here, and write down the Name of each *Sound,* (as in *pag.* 5.*)* underneath the *Note*; which shews its Station.

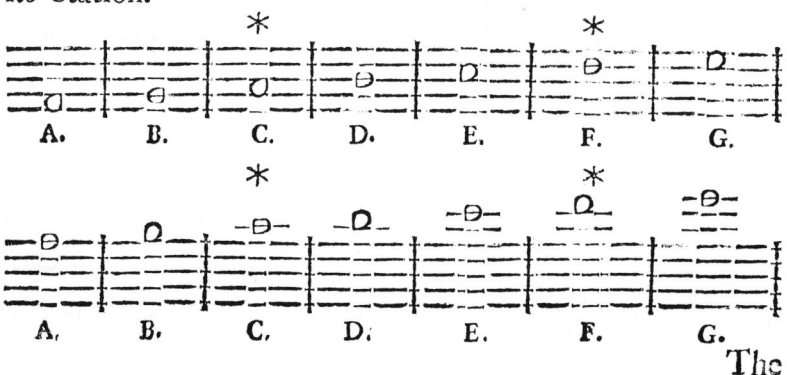

A.   B.   C.   D.   E.   F.   G.

A.   B.   C.   D.   E.   F.   G.

The

The uppermoſt of the two *Staff's* above, begins the Progreſſion from the Letter *A*, and carries it on, till you come to *G*; and the lowermoſt continues it on, in *Octaves* from *A* to *G* again. Thoſe with *Stars* over them, are the *Semitones*, formerly taken Notice of, (in *Page* 8.) which are *C* and *F*; the Reaſon for applying thoſe Letters to them, you will ſee preſently. This, naturally leads us to enquire a little farther into this Matter, it not being enough to diſtinguiſh the Names of *Sounds* by a Number of Letters only; but we muſt conſider alſo, of a proper Method to apply ſome other Names to them, ſuch as may naturally lead us to the true *Tone* of them, in ſinging them over; this being as material a Thing as any: For, it is undoubtedly true, (what an incomparable * Author hath ſaid) that *a Voice doth expreſs a* Sound *beſt, when it pronounceth ſome* Word *or* Syllable *with it.* To which Purpoſe, there have been ſeveral *Scales* formed; one, in one *Province*, and another, in another, &c. That, which the *Europeans* make uſe of, is the *Greek-Scale*, reduced into an eaſy Form by *Guido Aretinus*, a *Monk*, near 800 *Years* ago, who has rendered it much more commodious for the *Voice*, than it was before; (the Words being too long to pronounce in Singing, ſince the refining of *Muſick*) by adapting new Names, compiled out of ſix *Syllables*, from a *Hymn* (as Hiſtory relates) of St. *John* the *Baptiſt*; which are as follows, viz.

Ut, Re, Mi, Fa, Sol, La;
which ſix *Syllables*, he joyned to the ſeven *Letters* aforeſaid, and ſet them down in the following Form. (But, becauſe of the Difficulty the *Reader* may find in

pro-

---

* *See* Sympſon's Compendium, *pag.* 3. *Edit.* 5.

(32)

pronouncing them; (they being a little intricate to a *Beginner*) I shall write down their Names as they are pronounced, in a *Column* overagainst them; and also shew, (by a little *Dash* over the *Vowel*) where the *Accent* lies; which will be a great Help, if well minded. Observe also, that in *Ascending*, we reckon them forward; in *Descending*, backward.)

The SCALE.

Ffaut		*Effàut*
Ela		*èla*
Dlasol		*Deelàsol*
Csolfa		*Ceesòlfa*
Bfabemi		*Beefabèemi*
Alamire		*Alamìre*
Gsolreut		*Geesolrèut*
Ffaut		*Effàut*
Elami		*èlami*
Dlasolre		*Deelasòlre*
Csolfaut	Pronounced	*Ceesolfàut*
Bfabemi		*Beefabèemi*
Alamire		*Alamìre*
Gsolreut		*Geesolrèut*
Ffaut		*Effàut*
Elami		*èlami*
Dsolre		*Deesòlre*
Cfaut		*Ceefàut*
Bmi		*Bèemee*
Are		*àre*
Gamut		*Gàmut*

These

These Names thus clapt together, have no Manner of Signification in themselves; but are contrived for the Sake of *Order* and *Distinction* only, and answer the End of the Office for which they were intended, in every Circumstance; to wit, in expressing all the different *Tones* in the seven Degrees of *Sound*, (as whole *Tones*, and *Semitones*) to which they are applied. But here seems to be room for a Question, pertinent enough; which is, since there are seven different Degrees of *Sound*: Why are there not as many different *Syllables* applied to them? For as yet, we see but six. The Reason of this is, because there is no Occasion, even for six, though the *French*, to this Day, use seven: For, to the *Syllables* that we are here speaking of, viz. *Ut*, *Re*, *Mi*, *Fa*, *Sol*, *La*, they add another; which they call *Si*, (pronouced *See*) The *Syllables Ut* and *Fa*, being applied to the two *Semitones*; and *Re*, *Mi*, *Sol*, *La* and *Si*, to the others: But this is not accounted (by the *English*) so good a Method as we have practised, some *Centuries*, as finding it much easier, and more elegant to use no more than Four of these *Syllables*; which are *Mi*, *Fa*, *Sol* and *La*; the *t*, in the *Syllable Ut*, being too dead a *Mute* to express a *Sound* well, and the *R*, in *Re*, too harsh a *Liquid*; so, instead of *Ut*, we put *Fa*; for *Re*, *Sol*; and for *Si*, *Mi*; (pronounced *Mee*) the *Syllable Fa*, expressing a *Semitone* more naturally than any of the others, we apply it to both of them; and *Sol*, *La* and *Mi*, (the *Liquids* in them being smooth in Pronounciation) we apply to the whole *Tones*; so that *Mi* is repeated but once within the *Octave*, and the others twice; as *Fa*, *Sol*, *La*, *Fa*, *Sol*, *La*, *Mi*; or the *Mi* first: Or thus, *Fa*, *Sol*, *La*, *Mi*, *Fa*, *Sol*, *La*; according to the *Sound* from whence they begin their Progression, when they are supposed to ascend or descend gradually: For the better Explanation whereof, I shall set them down

down in the *Scale*, by repeating the same once again, with all their *Octaves*, in their true Position, represented by *Rising* and *Falling*.

Ffaut	——————————— Semitone	Fa ⎫
Ela		La ⎪
Dlasol	———————————————	Sol ⎪
Csolfa	Semitone	Fa ⎬ Treble.
Bfabemi	———————————————	Mi ⎪
Alamire		La ⎪
Gsolreut	——— 𝄞 —————————	Sol ⎫⎭
Ffaut	Semitone	Fa ⎪
Elami	———————————————	La ⎭
Dlasolre		Sol ⎫
Csolfaut	——— 𝄡 ——— Semitone	Fa ⎬ Tenor.
Bfabemi		Mi ⎪
Alamire	———————————————	La ⎫⎭
Gsolreut		Sol ⎪
Ffaut	——— 𝄢 ——— Semitone	Fa ⎭
Elami		La ⎪
Dsolre	———————————————	Sol ⎬ Bass.
Cfaut	Semitone	Fa ⎪
Bmi	———————————————	Mi ⎪
Are		La ⎪
Gamut	———————————————	Sol ⎭

Having thus informed you of the Reasons for applying these *Syllables*, in learning to tune the several Degrees of *Sound* vulgarly call'd *Sol-fa-ing*; it is requisite, in the next Place, to give you the meaning of the three different *Characters* placed in the middle of the *Scale*; upon the fourth *Line* of which, you find this Mark; 𝄢 which is called a *Cliff* or *Key*, from its opening to us the meaning of any thing, being commonly placed

upon

upon the fourth *Line* at the Beginning of each *Staff*, (according to what I obferved, *pag.* 31.) reckoning from the Bottom upward, and is proper to the *Bafs*, for which Reafon, it is called the *Bafs Cliff*, or otherwife, the *Ffaut Cliff*; the Firft, fignifying for what *Voice* any *Song* is compofed, and the Laft, the Names of the Places where the *Notes* lie, according to the Order of the *Scale*; for upon what *Line* foever this *Cliff* may happen to be placed, (it being, upon fome Occafions, (but very rarely) placed upon the third *Line*) that *Line* is called *Ffaut*; and the *Space* between that and the *Line* above it, *G folreut*; and fo of the reft, both above and below the *Cliff*, as you fee them lie in the *Scale*. Upon the fecond *Line* above that, you fee this *Mark*; which is occafionaly, placed upon either the third or fourth *Line*. If it be on the fourth; it is placed there to fignify that fuch a *Part* is for a *Tenor Voice*; if on the third, it then fignifies a *Contra-Tenor*, being varioufly placed, no otherwife than to keep the *Notes* within due *Bounds*, by hindering them from interfering with one another, according to the Compafs of either, *Voices*, or *Inftruments*. This *Cliff* is called in General, the *Tenor*, or *C folfaut Cliff*. Sometimes it is (and indeed, I think, ought always, in *Vocal Mufick*, to be) applied to the *Treble*, and then it ftands on the firft *Line* of each *Staff*. The Reafon why I would have this *Cliff* ufed for the *Treble* is, becaufe the *Notes* lie, fometimes pretty low, hardly leaving room for to write the Words underneath them, when they make ufe of the *Cliff* which ftands upon the fecond *Line* above this, in the *Scale*, and always placed upon the fecond *Line* of each *Staff*.

This *Cliff* is (as you fee) marked thus; and is cal-

F 2   led

led the *Treble Cliff*, or *G folreut Cliff*. There being no *Song*, or *Tune* whatever, but what has one of these *Cliffs* placed at the Beginning of each *Staff*; when we see them, we immediately know what Part it is.

There is yet one Thing that I should not here omit, which is to acquaint you that, in former Times the *Tenor Cliff* was as often placed upon the second *Line* as it was on any of the others, being called the *Mean Part*, but it is now wholly laid aside in Singing, except in *Cathedral Musick*, and very rarely in that, but for the *Organ* Parts; it is also pretty much used in *Instrumental-Musick*, as the *Tenor-Violin*, &c. but is never placed upon the fifth *Line*, neither for *Voices*, nor for *Instruments*.

You see in the *Scale*, the *Lines* arched in, by fives, which represent the *Staffs*, with all the different *Parts*, as *Treble*, *Tenor*, and *Bass*; and which, if you single them out, you will perceive the *Bass Cliff* to stand upon the fourth *Line*; the *Tenor-Cliff* on the third and the *Treble-Cliff*, upon the second *Line*. The *Scale* it self is called the *Gamut*, from the *Greek* Letter, *Gamma*, which *Guido Aretinus* placed at the Bottom, for no other Reason than to shew from whence he derived it, otherwise, it might have been more natural to have began with *Are*, in regard to the first Letter of the *Alphabet*; but as I observed, *pag.* 5. that *Musick* is not confined to any particular *Words*, or *Letters*; so is it meerly indifferent where we begin, any otherwise than for Form's Sake.

Having thus explained the *Scale* or *Gamut*, as the Seven Degrees of *Sound* lie, with their *Octaves*, shewing the several *Parts* for different *Voices*; I shall now give you an Example of each, in their proper Staffs, as they are used in Singing, with their Names writ underneath the *Note* that shews their Situation, beginning at *Gamut*.

T R E-

(37)

Treble.

Elami F G A B C D E F

Treble.

Cſolfaut D E F G A B C D

Mean.

Alamire B C D E F G A B

Contra-Tenor.

Ffaut G A B C D E F G

Tenor.

Dſolre E F G A B C D E

Base.

Gamut A B C D E F G A

All

(38)

All which, are comprehended in the following *Example*.

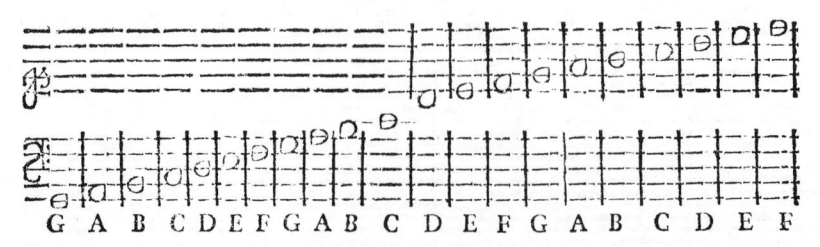

G A B C D E F G A B C D E F G A B C D E F

The Reason why the lowest *Part* is called the *Base*, and also, why the Uppermost is called the *Treble*, would be impertinent to repeat here, the Words being sufficient to explain themselves; and the *Tenor* likewise, one wou'd from its Name be naturally apt to conclude, that it always carried the Subject of the *Air*, when it is engaged with other Voices; and that was indeed, the Reason formerly, for calling it the *Tenor*: For, always laying next to the *Base*, they used to make it the prime *Part*; but People, in aftertimes, thought it more agreeable to let the highest *Part* bear the Subject, (since *Musick* has been so much improved, especially as it is at this Time) as being better heard; and consequently, easier distinguished: For a *Choir* of *Voices*, or a *Band* of *Instruments*, may be in this Case, compared to an *Army* drawn up in Order to *Battle*, where the Front of the *Platoons* shew themselves more immediately to the *Eye*, as the discharging their *Firelocks* has a more immediate Effect upon the *Ear*: So the better the Subject in a musical Performance is heard, the more pleasant it is; for if it were to be stiffled by the other *Parts*, it could not possibly have any good Effect at all. Yet notwithstanding this, the *Part* which lies next the *Base*, retains the Name of *Tenor* to this Day. It

may

may not be amifs to obferve to you, that, as the Word *Bafe* is derived from the *Latin* Word, *Baffus*; (which fignifies a *Foundation* or *Bafis*) fo they generally write *Bafs*, inftead of *Bafe*; which is an Abreviation of the Word *Baffus*, or the *Italian* Word, *Baffo*; which has the fame Signification.

I have one Thing more to fay, touching the *Scale* or *Gamut*; which is, that at firft, *i. e.* when the aforefaid Author, *Guido Aretinus*, reduced the *Greek Scale* into the Form which is now ufed, there was no *Sound* practifed above *Ela*; which gave Birth to the *Common-Proverb*, viz. *He Strains a* Note *above* Ela. But fince, they have added more, both for *Voices* and *Inftruments*, efpecially the *Violin*; which on fome Occafions, goes ten Degrees higher; and a *Treble-Voice*; fome of them three, and others four, according as *Nature* has caft them; for all *Voices*, though of the fame Kind, are not equally the fame, neither in Compafs, nor in Tone; which I have hardly any Occafion to fignify to thofe who have any tollerable *Ear* to *Mufick*. They have alfo defcended below *Gamut*; but it is very rare for a Compofer to contrive any Thing for a *Voice* to defcend above one Degree lower, though for *Bafe-Inftruments*, they go ftill lower, efpecially the *Organ*, fome of which are made to go a whole *Octave* lower; and for your better underftanding of which, I muft refer you back, to *pag.* 4. in what I faid, concerning the *Standard* of *Weights* and *Meafures*. Thofe *Sounds* above *Ela* are called, in *Alt*, which fignifies above; as *Ffaut* in *Alt*, *Gfolreut* in *Alt*, &c. and thofe below *Gamut*, are called *Double*; as *Double Ffaut, Double Elami*, and fo on, in the fame Order as you fee them lie in the *Scale*; which is very neceffary to be learned by Rote, both forward and backward, that you may be able at the firft View, to tell in what Place any *Note* ftands, in

all

(40)

all the *Cliffs*; without which, you can never know what you are about.

I would not have you imagin that I propose any Thing I can say here, in *Dead Letters*, to be sufficient to instruct you in the *Art* of *Singing*, without the Assistance of a *Living Tutor*: For if I did, it would be a gross Imposition upon you; for the Meaning of *Sounds* which we are unacquainted with, cannot be communicated to us without our hearing them: For as I formerly observed *(pag.* 2.) that *Sound* is not an Object of the *Eye*, &c. so it is impossible to give you any *Idea* of them in *Writing*, any otherwise, than to inform you in what Manner you are to apply them, after they are grown a little familiar to you. I send this abroad, only to inform, such as are under *Lame Guides*, how they may soon acquire more *Knowledge* in the *Science* of *Musick* than some of their *Masters*, by reading this Book; which is writ on Purpose to tell them the true Meaning of every Thing from *Natural Reason*; which I think, is the best Way of arguing, where we have Nothing else to depend upon, that can give us a competent *Knowledge* in what we are desirous to be informed of.

The first *Lesson* that we usually give to a *Learner*, (as being the most natural Way, serving as it were, for *Leading-Strings*) is the Seven plain Degrees of *Sound*, as they rise from the *Sound* given, in the *Gsolreut Cliff*, both ascencing and descending, as follows.

Sol la Mi fa sol la fa sol sol fa la sol fa Mi la sol

But

But, the properest Way is to begin at *Cfolfaut*; because (as I signified *pag.* 7.) the *major Seventh* being naturally required with the *major Third*, and F, being the *minor Seventh* to G, (*B*, being its *major Third*,) we ought not to balk the *Ears* of our *Pupils*, by contradicting the *Dictates* of *Nature*, and therefore ought to put it (rather in the *Cfolfaut Cliff*, where they will lie right.)

Thus.

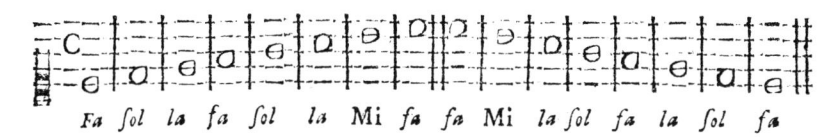

Fa sol la fa sol la Mi *fa fa* Mi *la sol fa la sol fa*

The *Gfolreut Cliff* may be, indeed, made use of; but then we shall be obliged to make an *Additional Line* below the *Staff*, when it may be avoided, if all our modern *Singing-Masters* (at least, such as are capable of it) would teach their *Scholars* (which is a very *Material Point*) to understand all the *Cliffs*, which very few of them do; and those that cannot, ought to betake themselves to some other Imployment. One cannot avoid being a little severe, while there is so much Occasion given to expose the *ridiculous Practises* of meer *Quacks* in *Musick*; which, I hope, I have effectually done, in the Discourse annexed to this Treatise. The best Way here, will be to give an *Example* in each of the *Cliffs*, that such as have a desire to know what they are doing, may not be left altogether in Ignorance.

(42)

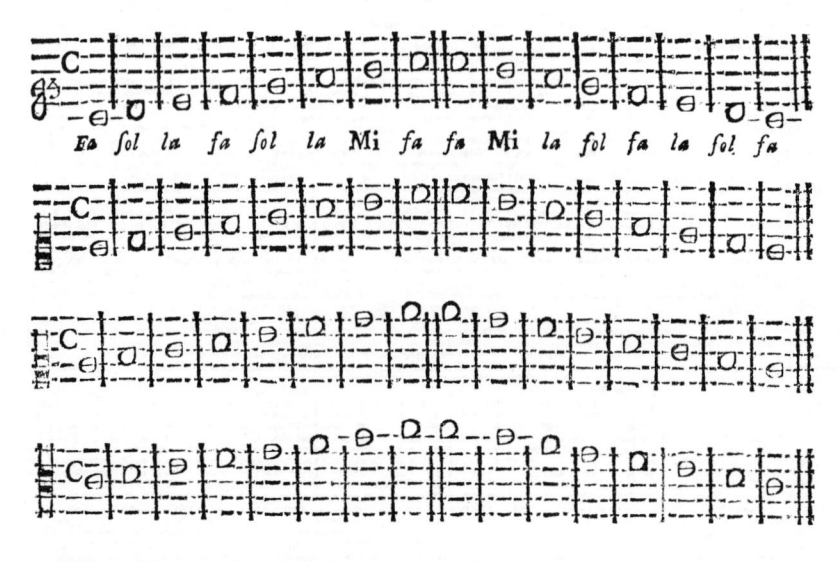

Fa sol la fa sol la Mi fa fa Mi la sol fa la sol fa

The *Tenor*, beginning an *Octave* lower, according to the Positions in the *Scale*.

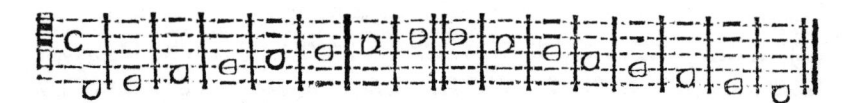

The *Base* in *Unison*, i. e. the same *Tone* with the *Tenor*.

It is here to be noted, (as you may see, by taking a View of the *Degrees* in the *Scale*, *pag.* 34.) that the four uppermost *Staffs* move together in the self-same *Tones*, (which we call *Unisons*) the Difference being only in the Situation of the *Cliffs*; and the two lowest
Staffs,

Staff's, viz. the *Tenor* and *Base,* move in *Unison* together an *Octave* below them, to prevent the making of too many *Additional Lines*; by which, you see the Necessity there is of having different *Cliffs,* and the various *Stations* of the *Tenor Cliff*; which I spoke of, *(pag.* 35.*)*

I think it a very proper (though not a customary) Way, after we have set our *Scholars* the eight *Notes,* as I have just now delivered them, to make them ascend a second Time, twelve.

Thus,

Fa   sol   la   fa   sol   la   Mi   fa   sol   la   fa   sol

and then, to descend back again,

Thus,

Sol   fa   la   sol   fa   Mi   la   sol   fa   la   sol   fa

Here we *Ascend* and *Descend,* in such a Manner, as seems to invite our *Ears* to attend these twelve *Notes*; for as we proceed, either upward or downward, we meet the *Perfect Concords* (*i.e.* the *Fifth* and the *Eighth*) so, as that the *Ear* cannot avoid being pleased with them by the Way, they appear so beautiful; and the more the *Ear* is regaled, the stronger will the Impression be, which they leave upon the *Memory*; and will therefore, be the more likely to dwell there: But before

fore we proceed to rife twelve Degrees, we muft take Care to be very perfect in the former *Example* of eight; for if we are imperfect in a fmall *Number*, it is not to be expected that we fhould improve upon a greater, where the one, is but an Introduction to the other; like *Numeration* in *Arithmetick*, where we muft learn to number *Hundreds* and *Thoufands*, before we come to *Millions*, &c.

And here, particular Care ought to be taken, in exerting the *Voice*, fo far as to hinder it from falling out of the *Key* we are fuppofed to begin in; which without a great deal of Caution ufed, it will be very apt to do, by little and little, fo infenfibly, that we fhall never be able to fing in *Tune*. To prevent which Inconvenience, we ought always to keep a *Scholar* to the *Standard* (or *Confort*) *Pitch*; which will certainly, the better enable him to remember the feveral *Tones* the more readily. To which End, to thofe who do not teach to fing by an Inftrument (as many do not) a *Pitch-Pipe* would be a very neceffary *Utenfil*, to be always carried about them.

When a *Learner* is perfect in the foregoing; we may proceed to give him the fame *Examples* in minuter *Notes*, to bring him by Degrees, to beat the *Meafures* true, as

Thus.

(45)
Thus.

After

After these, or such like, we may proceed to the former *Example* of twelve,
Thus,

and then break them, as you see,
Here,

(47)

As I have here given a few Examples of the Method that is to be taken, in Order to make a Man a *Singer*, by *Art*, as well as by *Nature*; so before I proceed any farther that Way, I think it convenient to inform you of some other Characters which are used, besides those I have already made you acquainted with; the first I shall observe to you, is the *Mark* of *Extension*, without which, we can never know when a *Sound* is to be extended, as in contracting of a *Sound*, a proper *Mark* is also as necessary, by the same Rule.

The *Mark* of *Extension* is called a *Sharp*; extending of a *Sound* being called in another Name, the sharpening of it. The *Mark* is this ; ♯ and is always placed on the left Side of the *Note* which is to be extended.

The *Mark* for *Contraction* is called a *Flat*; the contracting of a *Sound* being called the flattening of it. This *Mark* is thus ; ♭ which like the *Sharp*, is also placed on the left Side of the *Note*.

You are to observe, that when you see the *Sharp* placed before any *Note*, tho' it alters the *Sound* of it, yet the same *Syllable* is, still to be applied to it, as if there were no *Sharp* at all; but when you see the *Flat*, which commonly falls more immediately upon *Mi*, than any other *Note*, the Syllable *Fa*, expressing a *Semitone* (as I formerly told you) more naturally than either of the others, is to be applied to it, there not being so much Occasion to change the *Syllables* in the sharpened *Notes*, because the *Syllables Mi, Sol*, or *La*, are always applied to them, the *Sharp* being never placed to the *Mi*, (for the Reasons delivered in *pag.* 7) nor is the *Flat*, ever put to either of the two *Semitones*, to which the *Syllable Fa*, is applied, for the Reasons given in the same *Page*. Nor can we have the *Sharp* upon *Elami*, because the next above it (which is *Ffaut*) is but a *Semitone* to it. From all which, we must

naturally

(48)

naturally conclude, that the three *Sounds, viz.* the *Second, Fifth,* and *Sixth,* as mentioned, *Ibid.* which I told you were capable of being both extended and contracted, are *D, G,* and *A,* as in the following
Example.

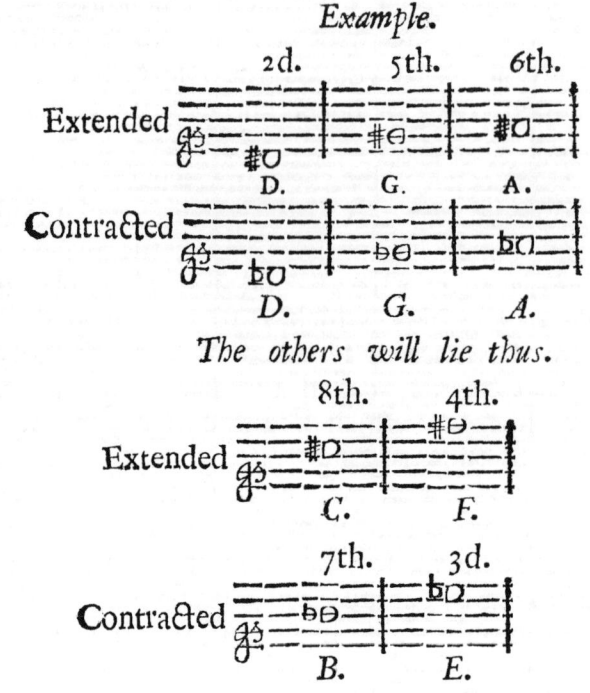

[Musical example showing Extended and Contracted forms of the 2d (D), 5th (G), and 6th (A).]

The others will lie thus.

[Musical example showing Extended 8th (C) and 4th (F); Contracted 7th (B) and 3d (E).]

Take all which together, both *Natural* and *Artificial,* in the *major,* and *minor Third*; they will appear
Thus.

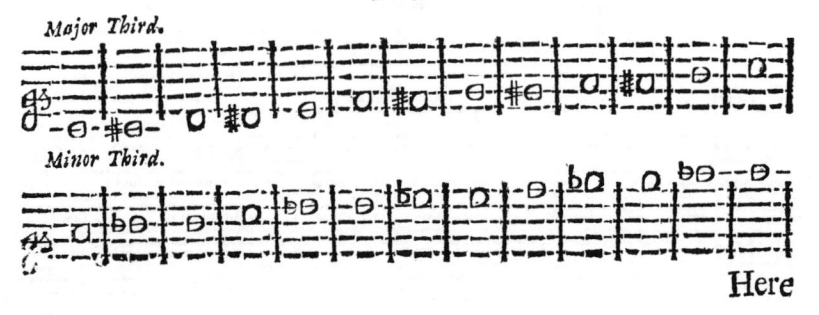

Major Third.

[Musical example]

Minor Third.

[Musical example]

Here

Here you see, in each *Staff*, the eight *Sounds* divided into twelve equal *Parts*, as I observed to you, *pag.* 7. that is to say, twelve *Semitones* from the *Sound* given, to the *Octave*; but these are not given you by Way of *Lesson*, in Order to tune them with your *Voice*; for the lowermost *Staff* is so very intricate, that a *Voice*, cannot well sound them in tune; and when we meet with any of them in any *Song* or *Lesson*; they come prepared for the *Ear*, by other *Notes* preceeding them, according to the *Fancy* or *Humour* of the *Composer*. I shall therefore give you an Example of the said twelve *Semitones*, as they lie in the lowermost *Staff*, expressed both by *Flat* and *Sharp*, in two *Staffs*, which are both of them in *Unison*, with respect to their Proportion, tho' of different Effects to the *Ear*.

Example.

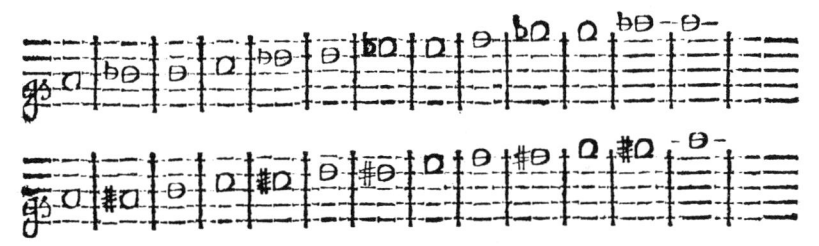

In the second *Bar* of the upper *Staff*, you see the *Flat* placed before B, which contracts the *Tone* of it half the Way towards A, underneath which, in the lower *Staff*, the *Sharp* is placed before A, which extends the *Tone* of the same, half the Way towards B, both which demonstrate to your View, the different Quality of each; and altho' they bear the same Proportion, yet are they different in Nature of *Sound*; for the extending of *Sounds*, make them yield a chearful *Tone* to the *Ear*; and when they are contracted, they appear Melancholly; which may be illustrated by the Comparison of different *Ideas*, in any Things that are supposed to *Rise*, or *Fall*, which needs no farther Explanation to those who understand the Distinction between being lifted up, and cast down, &c.

You see also in the first *Bar*, of the upper *Staff*, *D. Flat*, against *C. Sharp*; in the seventh *Bar*, *E. Flat*, against *D. Sharp*; in the tenth *Bar*, *G. Flat*, against *F. Sharp*; and in the twelfth *Bar*, *A. Flat*, against *G. Sharp*; all which have the same Proportion as *B. Flat*, and *A. Sharp*.

It is here again, further to be considered, that whenever the *Sharp*, or the *Flat* happens to fall on any *Note*; if the said *Note*, be immediately succeeded, by another, or more, tho' it be never so many, standing in the same Place where the *Sharp*, or *Flat* falls; they are all to have the same *Tone* given them as the First, unless contradicted; but when such *Notes* are succeeded by others, standing in different Places (as it often happens) and the former should be met with again, without either *Flat*, or *Sharp*; the said *Note*, is then to be sounded all one as if it never had been sharpened, &c. unless it be in the same *Bar*, where if it be required to have its former *Tone*; it has always this Mark; ♮ placed before it, which is called a *Natural*, or the *Mark* of *Restoration*, and is always used on such Occasions; though formerly, we had no such *Mark* in Use; nor is it yet, twenty Years ago since I first met with it; before which, the *Flat* was always made Use of to contradict the *Sharp*; and the *Sharp*, to contradict the *Flat*; which you will sometimes meet with still, all People not being, yet thoroughly acquainted with the true Use of the *Natural*, as not knowing how to apply it in all Cases, tho' there is nothing in *Musick*, more easy. The Use of the *Natural*, in the two foregoing *Staffs*, will make the uppermost stand Thus,

(51)
Thus.

which is much more Natural than to put *Sharps*, as

Thus.

or *Flats*, in the lowermost *Staff*, when reverſed, (there being no Occaſion for any as it is)

Thus.

the Reaſon for not admitting of which, is plain; for the *Sharp* being a *Mark* for abſolute *Extenſion*; and the *Flat*, the ſame for *Contraction*; (the *Natural* denoting neither) by applying either of them in the Caſe of *Reſtoration*, we contradict the original Intention of them, in making them act contrary to the Nature of their *Office*; and therefore the lowermoſt *Staff*, when reverſed, as above, ought to ſtand

Thus.

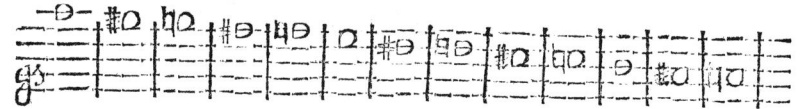

Having thus explained to you the true Nature of *Extenſion*, *Contraction*, and *Reſtoration*, under the *Characters* of *Sharp*, *Flat*, and *Natural*; I ſhall proceed to

(52)

to give you a few *Lessons* more; for as yet, you have had no more than two or three Examples, *Note* after *Note*, in a gradual Progression, by *Rising* and *Falling*; but these alone, will not avail much; without we are also made acquainted with the Distances of each of the seven Degrees of *Sound*, both in their natural *Situation*, and in the Capacity of their *Extension* and *Contraction*, &c. by *Skips* or *Leaps*, (as in *pag.* 2.) from the *Sound* given, which I shall first do, in their natural *Situation*, *i. e.* according to the plain *Scale*; and next agreeable to the *Chromatick*, according to what I mentioned *pag.* 6. (which, the two late Examples are a Specimen of) the first of which, take as follows.

Thirds.

Natural.

Continued.

Continued.

Fourths.

Fifths.

(55)

Fifths.

Sixths.

Sixths.

Sevenths.

(57)

Sevenths.

Eighths.

Eighths.

Thirds.

(59)

Thirds.

Fourths.

Fifths.

Sixths.

Sevenths.

(60)

Sevenths.

Eighths.

When you are pretty Perfect in these, you may proceed in the following Manner;

Thus.

Artificial.

fa Mi

It

It would be endless to attempt to give you all the ways of these *Bearings*, because, as I said *(pag. 13.)* their *Variation* is infinite, nevertheless, these, well practised, will sufficiently enable you to make a speedy Progress, with a diligent Application; for when once you come to make these *Tones* a little familiar to your *Ear*, you must take care to keep them in your *Memory* while they are warm, as we call it. I say, a diligent Application will soon bring you thoroughly acquainted with every thing that is necessary to be known in the *Art* of *Singing*. But there are yet, some other Things, material to be known, before you proceed any farther in tuning your Notes; for,

It being frequent, in Singing, or Playing in *Confort*, for one *Part*, or more, (as Occasion requires) sometimes, to pause, while the others continue in Motion; it is, therefore, necessary to have *Marks* of Distinction, to shew the Length of *Time*, that each *Part* is to stand still;

which

which *Marks* are diftinguifhed by the refpective *Notes*, or *Meafures*, that the others are performing, and are call'd *Refts* or *Paufes*, as follows.

NOTES with their RESTS.

The *Semibreve Reft*, you fee, is a full Stroke made underneath one of the five *Lines*, which fignifies that you are to paufe (or ceafe *Singing*) a whole *Meafure*, in any of the *Moods* in *Tripple-Time*, as well as in the *Common Moods*. The *Minim Reft* is made like that of the *Semibreve*, which is diftinguifhed from it by being made over the *Line*; this alfo denoting half a *Meafure*, in any of the *Moods* where the *Meafures* are equally divided, as in the *Mood* of $\frac{6}{4}$ $\frac{6}{2}$ and $\frac{3}{2}$, only in the *Common Mood* of $\frac{2}{4}$ half a *Meafure* is reprefented by the *Crotchet Reft*, as having but two *Crotchets* to a *Meafure*, which *Reft*, you fee is a *Figure* of *Seven* reverfed; the *Quaver Reft*, the *Figure* in its right Pofition; the *Semiquaver*, has a *Dafh* under the Head of the Figure, which anfwers to the double Stroke on the Tail of the *Note* which it reprefents; and the *Demiquaver*, you fee, has two *Dafhes* under the Head of the *Figure*, which anfwer to the *Tripple Stroke* on the *Tail* of its *Note*. When we are to paufe the Length of two *Semibreves*, (or *Barrs*) the *Reft* is brought down, quite to the next *Line* underneath; which I fhall here explain, as they are fuppofed to be Multiplied, tho' never fo many of them, and write their Numbers over the *Staff*.

When

(63)

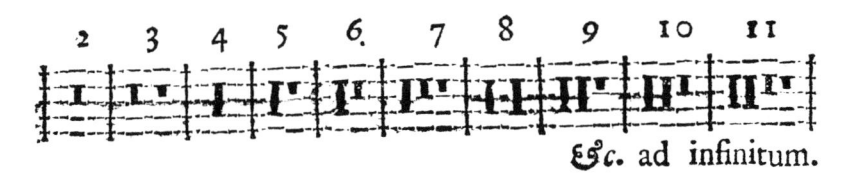

&c. ad infinitum.

When you see an *Arch* (which we call a *Slur*) over the Heads of two, or more *Notes*, thus; ⌒ or underneath thus; ‿ those *Notes* so arched in, are to be sung all in on *Vowel* or *Syllable*.

A double *Bar* ‖ signifies the End of a *Strain*, like a full *Point* or *Period*, at the End of a *Sentence*.

If it be pointed thus; ⁞‖⁞ it denotes the *Strain* to be repeated.

This *Mark*, :S: signifies a *Repetition*, too, but then it is only from the Place where it is set.

This *Mark* ⌘ is commonly set at the End of each *Staff*, for the Guide of the *Eye*, in performing any Thing at the first Sight of it, to direct us where the first *Note* of the next *Staff* stands; for which Reason, it is called a *Director*.

The most difficult Thing to a *Beginner*, in beating the *Measures*, is in such *Notes* as we call driving *Notes*, where we beat with the *Hand*, or *Foot*, in the Middle of a *Sound*, or *Note*, that shews the Length of it, and at the next *Note*, lift it up again. This was formerly practised, by drawing the *Bars* thro' the Heads of such *Notes*, before *Crotchets* and *Quavers* were in Use; for which Reason, they were then called *Notes* of Syncopation, which signifies cutting.

Ex-

(64)

Example.

But this Way is less perplexing to the *Eye* as follows.

The same *Example* may be put in minuter *Notes*, which oblige the *Hand* to be down, in the Middle of one *Note*; and up, in the Middle of the following.

Thus.

or Thus.

The same *Example* explained, by dividing it into *Crotchets*.

which, without driving, will appear,

Thus

(65)

Thus.

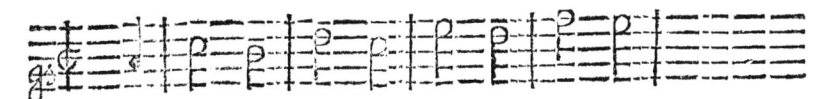

The Reason for thus driving of *Notes* is, that they have a particular Beauty in them, in some Sort of *Musical Compositions*, both *vocal* and *instrumental*; therefore I shall give you a *Lesson* or two that Way, to bring you a little acquainted with them.

When you have once master'd this *Lesson*, you will be the better able to beat it in other *Notes*; in which, you have but half the Number of *Measures*, as follows,

Example.

Explained.

Explained.

If you practise this last well, without taking in the *Slurs*; you will find it much easier afterwards, to sing them as they are intended; the better to facilitate which, I shall here set the last *Example* down again, the Way that I would have you do it, that you may not mistake my Meaning.

After this, you may practise the same *Lesson* over again, with *Rests*,

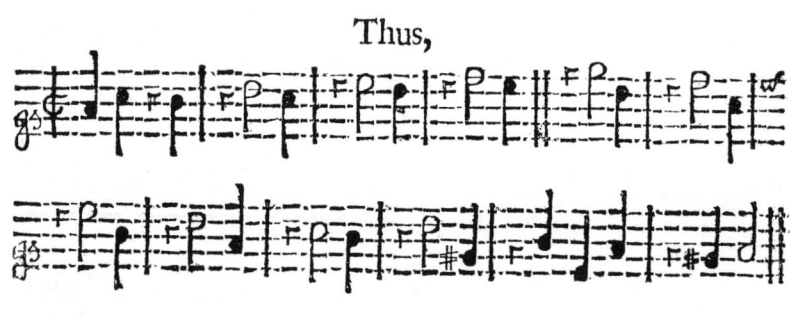

Thus,

I would

(67)

I would set down more *Lessons* of this Kind, but then they would so discourage a *Learner*, as to make him almost despair of ever being a *Singer*; for it is not the *Eye* that we are altogether to feed, but the *Ear*; and whoever does but once get the Mastery over those that have been here already pointed out for him, he cannot fail of executing any Thing of the same Kind that he shall meet with, if he take but that Care which is requisite; *i. e.* not to be overhasty and impatient to run upon the full Trott before he can Amble well, it being the Way of all *Beginners*, in all *Arts* whatever; for which Reason, I thought this CAUTION absolutely necessary.

In the next Place, I shall give you a *Lesson* in each of the *Moods* in *Tripple-Time*; after which, I shall lay down some general *Rules* that I have not yet treated of, and which will finish this Treatise.

Three times *One*.
In the *Mood* of *Three* to *Two*.

K 2 The

(68)

The *Mood* of *Three* from *Four*.

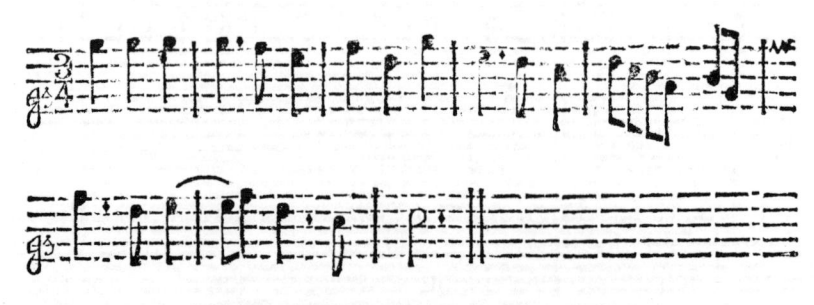

The *Mood* of *Three* from *Eight*.

Three times *Three*.
In the *Mood* of *Nine* to *Four*.

The

(69)

The *Mood* of *Nine* to *Eight*.

Two times *Three*.
In the *Mood* of *Six* to *Four*.

The *Mood* of *Six* from *Eight*.

Four

Four times *Three*.
In the *Mood* of *Twelve* to *Eight*.

Of Transposition.

IN the Case of *Transposition*, which is to remove any *Song* or *Tune*, so many *Notes* or *Sounds* higher or lower, than what they were supposed to be before; and which is frequently done, both for *Voices* or *Instruments*, agreeable to what I observed *(pag. 4.)* concerning the Relation of different *Sounds*, joyned together upon the same *Basis*. In this Case, I say, we are to distinguish between the *major* and *minor Third*; for all Kind of *Musick* whatever, has its Dependance upon one of these *two*, which are occasionally removed out of their natural Places; sometimes by a *Flat* or more (according as Occasion requires) placed before the *Cliff*, in every *Staff* of such *Songs* or *Tunes* as they are employed in; which signifies that all the *Notes* that fall in any of those Places where the *Flat* or *Flats* stand, are to be sung or played flat; unless (as it often happens) contradicted by the *Natural*. Sometimes by one, or more *Sharps*, which also oblige all such *Notes* to be

sung,

sung, or played sharp, &c. and when any of these appear, the *Names* of the *Notes* in *Sol-fa-ing* are likewise changed, according to the Number of *Flats* or *Sharps*, that shall happen to be placed before the *Cliff*. These Things being considered, it now remains that I give you an Account how such *Flats* and *Sharps* are introduced, according to the natural *Situation* of *Tones*; which will also shew how the Name of each is changed by them.

You may easily gather, from what I have already observed to you, of the natural Capacity of each of the seven Degrees of *Sound*, that there are but five of them, to wit, A, B, D, E and G, that will admit of a *Flat*; and five also, to wit, A, C D, F and G, that will admit of a *Sharp*. But, there being variety sufficient on all Occasions, in four of each; the *Flat* is never placed, in this Case, before G; nor the *Sharp*, before A; though on some Occasions they are both made use of, by Way of interveining, but never placed at the *Cliff*, at least, not in *Vocal Musick*; so that I need only to give you an Account of four of each, which will be sufficient for your Purpose.

You are first to take Notice, (as you may see in the foregoing *Examples*) that when the *Third* to the *Key* is the *greater* (which we call the *Sharp*) *Third*; according to what I said, (*pag.* 6.) then, *Cfaut* is the *Key*. If the *Third* to the *Key* be the *Lesser* (or *Flat*) *Third*; then *Are* is the *Key*. So, that let the Number of *Flats* or *Sharps* be what they will, we can form but two *Keys* in each of them, *viz.* the *Sharp Third* and the *Flat Third*; between which two *Keys*, the *Mi* (by which the rest are governed) is always placed; and let it be where it will, the others remove along with it, as its *Train* of *Attendants*, like *Jupiter* and his *Satellites*. And first, I shall speak of the *Flat*.

As

As I have here obferved, that the *Syllables Fa, Sol* and *La* are to accompany the *Mi*, wherefoever it is removed; fo the *Flat* falls immediately upon the fame, in all fuch Variations; and the Reafon for this is, becaufe as its firft natural *Place* is in *Bmi*, which is the *major* (or *fharp*) *Seventh* to *C faut*, it requires the *Flat* to fall, more immediately there; for if we were to place it firft any where elfe, it could not be proper; for fuppofing we were to put a *Flat* in *Elami*; this would then, become a *defective Fourth* to *Bmi*, which would create four whole *Tones*, fucceffively in the *Octave, viz.* F, G, A and B, which *Nature* never conftituted; and if we place it firft upon *Dfolre*, this would bring two *Semitones* together, *viz.* C and D, which is alfo unnatural; the *Second* above it, which is E, would alfo become a whole *Tone* and half to it; which is alfo, contrary to *Nature*, as being but one Degree above it; for a whole *Tone* is the greateft Diftance in a *Second*, in its natural *Situation*; and if we place it in *Are*, then B would become a whole *Tone* and one half from it, which would bear the fame Proportion as the putting the *Flat* in *Dfolre*; nor can we place it in *Gamut*; becaufe this would alfo, create two *Semitones* together, which are F and G, the fame in Proportion, as if we were to place it in *Dfolre*, and would alfo make A, a whole *Tone* and half to it. From whence it plainly appears, that the firft Place the *Flat* comes into, muft be *Bmi*, or its *Octave*; for whatever *Sound* is flattened or fharpened; the fame is to be underftood of its *Octave*, both above and below it. And when the *Flat* is thus placed in B, it makes E (which is the *Fourth* above it) become the fame, in Proportion, as B in the natural *Scale*; and accordingly, removes the *Mi* up, into E. After this, natural Reafon informs us, that its next Place is in A, (B and E, being

ing both flattened) which is the *Fourth* above E. The next in D, (B, E and A being flattened) which is the *Fourth* above A; and its fourth and last Place in G, (B, E, A and D, being all four flattened) which is the *Fourth* above D.

The first Place that the *Sharp* comes into, is *Ffaut*; for if we Place it first of all, in *Cfaut*; it makes F, which is its *Fourth* above, become an *imperfect Fourth* to it; which is not allowable, for the same Reason that excludes the *Flat* from coming first into *Elami*; nor will any other Place besides *Ffaut*, first admit of it; as you may easily perceive, by what has been already said of placing the *Flat*. I shall set you down a short *Lesson* in each of the *Keys* we have been speaking of, and then come to a Conclusion. Only observe by the Way, that wherever the *Sharp* falls, the *Mi* is removed into the same Place; as when it comes into F, there put your *Mi*. When it comes into C, (which is its second *Place*) place it there. When into G, (which is its third *Place*) place it there. And when it comes into D, (which is its Fourth and last *Place*) place the *Mi* there. Here follow *Examples*.

Sharp Thirds.

C: *Natural.* Mi *in* B.

G : *Sharp.*

(74)

G : *Sharp.* Mi *in* F.

D : *Sharp.* Mi *in* C.

A : *Sharp.* Mi *in* G.

E : *Sharp.* Mi *in* D.

F : *Natu-*

(75)

F: *Natural.* Mi *in* E.

B: *Flat.* Mi *in* A.

E: *Flat.* Mi *in* D.

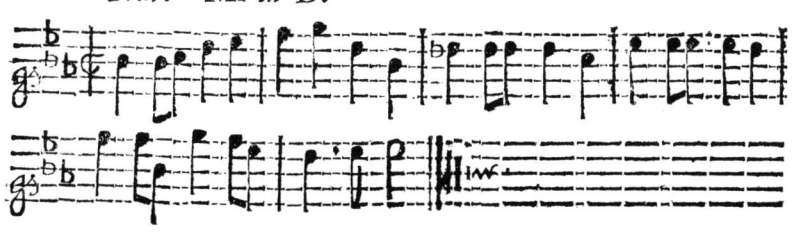

A: *Flat.* Mi *in* G, *never us'd.*

L 2 *Flat*

(76)

Flat Thirds.

A: *Natural.* Mi *in* B.

E: *Natural.* Mi *in* F.

B: *Sharp.* Mi *in* C.

F: *Sharp.* Mi *in* G.

C: *Sharp.*

(77)

C: *Sharp.* Mi *in* D, *never us'd.*

D: *Natural.* Mi *in* E.

G: *Flat.* Mi *in* A.

C: *Flat.* Mi *in* D.

F: *Flat.*

F: *Flat.* Mi *in* G.

In the two laſt *Bars*, in F. *Sharp*, you may perceive the *Sharp* to be placed upon E. And alſo, in the two laſt *Bars*, in C. *Sharp*, it is placed on B. Both which ſeem to contradict what I ſaid, in *pag.* 47. But then it is to be underſtood, that this is done by Way of borrowing; for F. being extended in the firſt, and C. in the other, leaves room for E. and B. to encroach as it were, by thruſting themſelves into their Neighbours Places: And as long as it is regular, it is ſo far excuſable, for where there is any Scope left, a Compoſer ought not to baulk his Fancy, out of a timorous Fear of tranſgreſſing againſt *Nature*'s Laws, where ſhe is not abuſed; for when we have Occaſion to borrow, her liberal Hand is always extended, if we do not joſtle her; for though we are allowed to borrow, in the Caſe before us; yet we are not to make uſe of extream *Sharps* or *Flats*, to form a *Key* in, the Reaſon for which is as plain as any Thing whatever. For ſuppoſe any one had a Fancy for compoſing an *Air* in F. with a *Flat* before it; this would in good Soberneſs, be nothing more than E. &c. The like may be ſaid of A. and B. both which demonſtrate what I ſaid in *pag.* 7. to be found Doctrine.

There

There yet remains one Thing that I ought to take some Notice of, before I take my leave of you, it being as material almost, as any Thing I have hitherto treated of; and of which many heavy Complaints have been made, and I believe always will be, if some Care be not taken to instruct People, how to understand that which very few have any true Notion of, and all for want of being well grounded at first, it being impossible for those who learn things by halfs, to understand any Thing thoroughly.

The Thing which I am speaking of, is a common Complaint against most Composers of *Musick*, who are very much blamed, (I will not say with what Reason) for the Omission of (now and then) a *Flat* or a *Sharp*, which they ought to place before the *Cliff*. And all this *Squabble* proceeds from the want of knowing where to place the *Mi* in those Extremities; for suppose a *Song* to be set in D, *natural*, which requires a *Flat* in B, and there happens to be no *Flat* there, but what is put before such *Notes* as fall in that Place: Now we all know, that when there is neither *Flat* nor *Sharp*, placed before the *Cliff*, the general Rule is to place the *Mi* in B: But then, the Key must be either, A, *natural*, or C, *natural*; if it be E, *natural*; G, *sharp*; D, *natural*, or F, *natural*; though there be no *Flat* nor *Sharp*, placed at the *Cliff*; yet one, or the other, is supposed to be there; for when they are omitted at the *Cliff*, they are always placed before the *Notes*, as aforesaid. Therefore, if a *Song*, or *Tune*, end in D, or F; the *Mi* is in E, and a *Flat* supposed in B. If it end in E or G: the *Mi* is in F, and a *Sharp* supposed to be there.

Again,

Again, when there is a *Sharp* in F, and the laſt *Note* in B or D; there is then a *Sharp* required in C, and the *Mi* is there.

When F and C, are both ſharpened, and the laſt *Note* fall in A or F; there is then a *Sharp* required in G, and the *Mi* is there.

If F, C and G, are all three ſharpened, and the laſt *Note* fall in E; then there is a *Sharp* required in D, which obliges the *Mi* to be there.

Next, when there is a *Flat* in B, and the laſt *Note* in B or G; a ſecond *Flat* is then required in E, and the *Mi* is in A.

When B and E, are both flattened and the laſt *Note* fall in C, or E; there is then a *Flat* required in A, and the *Mi* is in D.

Laſtly, when B, E and A, are all three flattened, and the laſt *Note* fall in F; then there is a *Flat* required in D, and the *Mi* is in G.

As to *Shakes*, *Beats*, *Back-falls*, &c. which ſome Authors have treated of, I find it to no Manner of Purpoſe to give any Account of them; for to thoſe who cannot take them by *Nature*, all *Human Art* is loſt, and all other Things in this *Science* will prove ineffectual.

FINIS.

To those who have learned to sing tollerably well in ye Treble Cliff in all the Variations of Sharps and Flats, the following Scheme will be very usefull being formed on purpose to shew them where the Mi lies, in all the other Cliffs tho' they have never been instructed in them, by applying each of them to the Treble, as follows.

Note, where the Mi is supposed, I have placed the Semibreve.

On the ABUSE OF MUSICK.

AS *Musick* hath been of late, very much worried, even to Death and Destruction, by many who through the want of a competent Knowledge thereof, have egregiously imposed on such as are ignorant of it; so it is thought as convenient to paint the *Pictures* of such, in as lively an *Image* as a *Pen* is capable of expressing.

If any one sees his own *Figure* here; and should chance to be scared at the hideous *Aspect* of his own wretched *Deformity*; his best Way will be to amend his *Deficiencies*; or if he wants a Capacity to do so; to throw off his *Pretensions* to what is not in his Power, ever to attain to.

As I am not fond of *Satyr*; I hope, none will accuse me with *Malice* in what I am going to inform them of. With *Envy*, I think they cannot, for I shall speak of none who may be justly, thought Objects thereof, but such only, as have rather, Matter for *Envy* themselves.

The first of these *Pretenders* to what they know nothing (or at best, but very little) of, are those who set up (some of 'em, with a modest Air of *Assurance* enough) for Composers of *Musick*, having a little Smattering thereto, by forming of some light *Airs*, which are the wild *Flirts* of an irregular Fancy, not at all digested for want of *Skill*; and which, when done, they procure some one or other of superior Talents to patch up an ill-favour'd *Visage*, by setting of *Bases*, Second *Trebles*, &c. to such unsavory *Productions*; after which, those People of extrajudicious Judgment, pass for *Masters* of *Musick*, by getting their Names affixed in *Print*, to their Performances; which in reality are not their own: For he's but an indifferent Workman, who after he has cut out a suit of Cloaths, knows not how to joyn the Pieces together; which, when done by another Hand, cannot be call'd his own Work. I would have my *Readers* note by the Way, that I condemn not any, meerly for their want of Judgment, but only such, as have *Vanity* enough to be thought *Artists*, in a *Science* which is as foreign to them as *Rhetorick* to a *Bear*. Nay, I have a particular Knowledge of some, who have taken extream Delight in being complimented with the Title of *Masters* of *Musick*, when they know not so much as the *Gamut*; just the same, as if a Man should acquire the Name of an experienced *Sailor*, who cannot say his *Compass*: A *Ship* would be well steer'd by such a *Pilot*. But, which is worst of all, these People, by such an unmerited Reputation, gain

Proselytes

Proselytes too, under the Pretence of teaching them to sing (miserably enough) and so pick their *Pockets*, as it were, of their *Money*. Pity it is, that such a lamentable *Disease* should want a *Remedy*. But this not being the only Grievance that wants redress, we must content ourselves with it, as well as we can; and those who Part with their *Coin* to purchase meer *Air*, we may blame, but not Pity; though they wasted even their whole Substance, on such *Trifles* of *Tutors*.

I am very willing to grant all that can be reasonably desired, in favour of those who (though they are never so deficient) do not *Ixion*-like, attempt to grasp at what they are conscious to themselves is beyond the Reach of their Capacity, and instead of a *Juno*, embrace an airy *Phantom*. But as to such as are thirsting after imaginary Waters, **W**hose aspiring Thoughts would soar to the top of *Parnassus* (tho' they have no taste of the Streams of *Helicon*) and exalt them above the *Muses*; I say, as to such, if we dipt our *Pens* in *Styx*, we could never be too severe upon them; for what can be more ridiculous than to see an *Ape* or a *Monkey*, dress'd up in rich embroider'd Apparel, when they know not how to wear it, and would be more apt to rend it to Pieces?

We all know, that to learn to read and write, are necessary Accomplishments for all Mankind; yet these alone, are not sufficient to qualify a Man to commence *Master* of *Arts*, &c. for which the *Sciences* of *Grammar*, *Logick* and *Rhetorick* must be well understood, and thoroughly digested; and for which also, the *English Tongue* alone, is not sufficient; for a Man may read very fluently, &c. and yet be an utter Stranger to all these, without which, he can never understand, even his own native *Language*. So is it in *Musick*; for,

To be a *Master* of *Notes*, is one Thing; and to be a *Master* of *Composition* is another. Let those then, who have not a Capacity for the latter, content themselves with keeping in their own *Sphere*; for he that is able to perform his Part in *Consort*, (without using fantastical Embellishments) need not gape for vain Praise, in desiring to be thought a greater *Artist* than he is; for a good Performer, (while he keeps within the Bounds of *Modesty*) is not unworthy the Esteem of Persons of the highest Rank; but for such as would jump out of their own *Element*; they must, like a *Fish* that leaps above the *Surface* of the *Water*, expect to fall again, to their proper *Centre*.

Another Sort of these *Fain-wou'd-bes*, are such as will shew a clever *Finger* upon the *Violin* or *Flute*, &c. and though they have Dexterity of Hand enough, when they perform singly; yet when they come to play their *Parts* in *Consort*, (though they are never so good Timists) they are so far from doing Justice, that they quite destroy the Subject of what they play, by their ridiculous out-of-the-way *Flourishes*, which is what we call murdering of *Musick*; and all to shew how nimbly they can tire an *Instrument* to Death: Just like some *Singers*, who (though many of 'em perform at the first Sight) are extremely fond of being heard to rattle in the *Throat*, though at the same Time, they banter both the *Musician* and the *Poet*, having Regard to neither *Sounds* nor *Words*, like a clumsey *Painter*, that casts false *Shades* to every Thing he draws; which is a most abominable *Abuse* of two noble *Arts*.

Were I of an ill-natur'd Temper, I could expose some Peoples Names, who have gain'd a great deal of undeserv'd Reputation, only by singing and playing downright Nonsense, and who will also, (perhaps) carry their Fame into the close *Mansions* of *Tellus*. Pity it
is

(5)

is, that they make not a better Use than they do, of those natural Talents with which they are endowed, for there wants only a little serious Application to make several of them deservedly famous. I would have them consider also, that a Man may write a very fine Hand, and yet be far from writing good Sense; or indeed, plain *Orthography*.

The real Cause of all this *Mischief* is, the want of good *Tuition*; for (according to what I formerly observed in the foregoing *Treatise*) it is not to be expected that all *Pupils* should exceed their *Tutors*. I could also, name some, who have had all the Advantages that can be desired, by learning of the greatest *Masters* that our *Isle* has produced; and yet are as far from observing their *Doctrine* as if they had never been instructed at all; notwithstanding that *Nature* has been as liberal to them as to any: But this proceeds from a *Laziness* of *Temper*; for when once they are qualified to teach People *Tune* and *Time*, they think they have gone far enough, and never trouble themselves with seeking for *hidden Treasure*, which is never to be discover'd by those who look no farther than the *Surface* of Things. I believe, there is hardly any Body that will Question the Truth of what I am going to say, (at least, those who are Judges) *viz*. I have heard several common *Ballad-Singers*, and common *Scrapers*, that have fidled before the *Bears*, do a *Song* or a *Tune* more Justice than a great many that have been nursed at the Feet of *Apollo*.

There are another Sort of pretty *Puppets*, who are some of 'em, dexterous enough, in playing upon the *Harpsicord*, &c. and understand *Composition* tolerably well; and so well, as to imagin that the little Knowledge they have acquired, is wholly owing to the good natured and communicative Temper of the *Instrument*:
And

And they are so well assured of this, that they'll hardly allow a possibility for such as are Strangers to the Method of playing on it, to have any Knowledge at all; though there are (you may venture for once to take it upon my own Word and Authority) some who are many Degrees superior to them. But who can resist an Authority of such Weight, which can give *Speech*, (without the Assistance of *Divine Illumination*) to Things inanimate? And here, I hope, I shall not give any Offence to my Friends amongst the *Papacy*, in saying, that this wild Notion is altogether as absurd, as *Transubstantiation*.

If you are curious, I'll inform you how you shall know (some at least of) these *irrational* reasonable *Animals*, by giving you a short Description of them, *viz.*

Sometimes, when they hear a Piece of *New Musick* perform'd, though it be never so good, you shall see them look, as it were, asquint; very sheepishly. Then ask, *Mr. a, how do you like this?* In answer to which, if they don't downright condemn it, they'll cry, (with an airy *Nod*, or a little *Shake*, with their empty Skulls.) *Why ——— truly, it's pretty good; tollerable enough.* And sometimes, *Troth, its* (with a strong affected Emphasis) *very good; really admirable! he has a good Genius, Faith and Troth; it's a thousand Pities that he does not play a little, upon the* Harpsicord, &c. Then ask them again, *Why Mr. a, what's playing on the* Harpsicord *to* Composition? Then they answer ye, (very earnestly, as if they verily believed what they say themselves) *Oh! bless me! that People should be so ignorant! Why that's all in all; for a Man can never understand* Composition, *unless he's a Perfect* Master *of the* Harpsicord; *for that's the only Thing that can instruct a Man,* &c. This plainly demonstrates, that

Harpsicords,

Harpsicords, &c. are unintelligible-intelligible *Agents* dropt from above, and sent hither by *Apollo*, on purpose to instruct poor ignorant *Mortals* in what they can never know, without it. One may very justly conclude, that if the *Harpsicord* had been in use, among the ancient *Heathens*, and they had entertain'd the same Notions of it as some of our modern (shall I call them) *Christians?* they would have broke down all their *Wooden Gods*, and have deified this in their room.

There are yet some other Matters that I might here take Notice of; but as I have already, exceeded the Length which I at first, designed this Book; I shall defer them to another Opportunity.

FINIS.